Easy Writing Skills
STEP-BY-STEP

Master High-Frequency Skills
for Writing Proficiency—*FAST!*

Ann Longknife, Ph.D., and K.D. Sullivan

New York   Chicago   San Francisco   Lisbon   London   Madrid   Mexico City
Milan   New Delhi   San Juan   Seoul   Singapore   Sydney   Toronto

1 2 3 4 5 6 7 8 9 10 11 12 13 14 15   QFR/QFR   1 9 8 7 6 5 4 3 2 1

ISBN   978-0-07-177451-2
MHID   0-07-177451-3

e-ISBN   978-0-07-177452-9
e-MHID   0-07-177452-1

Library of Congress Control Number   2011928671

Interior artwork by Newgen Imaging Systems

McGraw-Hill books are available at special quantity discounts to use as premiums and sales promotions or for use in corporate training programs. To contact a representative, please e-mail us at bulksales@mcgraw-hill.com.

Other titles in the series:
Easy Grammar Step-by-Step, Phyllis Dutwin

This book is printed on acid-free paper.

Contents

Acknowledgments

We'd like to thank Grace Freedson, our diligent literary agent, for her continued support, for her creative thinking, and for keeping us in mind for great projects; the entire McGraw-Hill editorial team for their guidance and dedication to high quality, with an extra thank-you to Andrea Coens for her superb copyediting expertise; and a special thank-you to Casey Dyson for his incredibly valuable insights and contributions.

Introduction

"I can't believe it," moaned Jean. "The first week of school and I've already been assigned an essay. There goes my grade—I've never been good at writing essays."

Jean is not the only student to feel this way. Most do. But wait! This difficulty can be overcome. Though writing is easier for some than others, it's important to know that *anyone* can write well! It takes planning and hard work, but writing is a skill, and like any other skill it involves learning the steps, learning how to apply those steps—and lots of practice.

We take you, step-by-step, through the writing process: from generation of ideas, through organization of those ideas, to production of a finished essay, you will improve your ability to think, to reason, and to communicate.

When you learn a new computer program or work to improve an athletic skill, you learn one step at a time and then build on and practice what you've learned to get better and better. You can use the same process to proudly climb the ladder to success and produce a well-written essay.

It takes certain steps to produce an effective essay, but it takes a solid foundation before you can get to the finished product. After all, you don't want to fall down and hurt yourself. So, we'll give you a good grip on each step, telling you what you need to know and what you need to do, so you can climb each step without slipping. During the climb, we'll also give you some tools to help you along the way.

An essay is a short piece of writing that develops a point in a clear, well-developed manner. You might want to describe how exotic you found Thailand, what you enjoyed about the book you read, or why one computer is better than another. Whatever the point you want to make, you want to logically and clearly lead your reader to understand your point.

One reason for writing an essay, of course, is because your teacher has assigned one. You'll write lots of essays during your school years. Knowing how to write an effective essay will get you better grades.

Beyond better grades, in all aspects of your life—work, volunteering, school—learning, decision making, and communicating are important. The real value of learning to organize is that it can help you think more clearly and present your ideas in a way that a reader can understand more readily. This applies to many types of communicating—perhaps at work to suggest a better way to perform a task, or in a letter to an editor debating a point. Even if it's in the form of an e-mail, you still want it well organized.

To help you get from the ground where you are standing to the top of the ladder—a well-written, finished essay—we'll provide you with the tools you need and show you, step-by-step, how to achieve your goal. We do not intend to make this a grammar book. We do include information that makes a difference in how well you're understood. Therefore, each chapter is a step up the ladder or a tool to help you in getting to the top.

- **Chapter 1, The Foundation.** The foundation of the writing process is knowing what an essay is, what it aims to do, and how to put it together effectively. This chapter discusses reasons for writing and the basic terms and concepts you'll need in beginning the writing process. It gives you a solid foundation on which to stand as you climb the ladder of writing an A+ essay.

- **Chapter 2, Getting Started, Step 1: Narrow Your Focus and Determine Your Thesis Statement.** Often, the hardest part of any assignment is getting started. This first step teaches you valuable ways to narrow your focus in choosing the subject of your essay and how to develop an effective thesis statement.

- **Chapter 3, Methods of Development, Step 2: Choose Your Method of Development.** Depending on the result you hope to achieve, you can use various methods of writing called *methods of development*. This step explains the various ways you can present your ideas, why each method is valuable, and which method is most ideal depending on whether your goal is to inform, to explain, or to persuade your reader.

- **Chapter 4, Form a Plan: Outlines, Step 3: Develop Your Outline.** Once you have chosen a topic and method of development for an essay, you need a plan—an outline—so you can present your ideas clearly. This step helps you organize your ideas using one of three outline styles and introduces the easy 1-2-3 method of planning an essay.

- **Chapter 5, Craft Your First Draft, Step 4: Write Your First Draft.** The standard essay consists of these required elements: title, an introductory paragraph—ending in a clear thesis statement—three developmental paragraphs, and a concluding paragraph. Having taken the steps to this point, next comes a big step up, as you take the information you've gathered to develop the key essay elements and produce a working draft that you can then craft into a finished essay.

- **Chapter 6, Your Writer's Toolbox: Sentences, Step 5: Prepare for Your Final Draft, Part 1.** Part of the process of refining your first draft is to examine each word, sentence, and paragraph to ensure what you've written is correct, clear, concise, and compelling. Chapters 6, 7, and 8 aren't steps up, but in them are the tools you'll need to help refine your writing. Review the information in these chapters in advance of sitting down to prepare your final draft. In this chapter you'll learn how to develop well-crafted sentences and how to avoid possible errors.

- **Chapter 7, Your Writer's Toolbox: Mechanics, Step 5: Prepare for Your Final Draft, Part 2.** This is your second set of tools. In this chapter we take a brief look at spelling, punctuation, and grammar and how some simple rules can ensure that your sentences are written correctly.

- **Chapter 8, Your Writer's Toolbox: Style, Step 5: Prepare for Your Final Draft, Part 3.** This third set of tools helps you elevate your writing to a higher level. Style is the combination of the words you use and the way you put them together. Just as we dress in our own style, we write in our own style. In this chapter, you'll learn some of the "tools of the trade" to give your writing flair, as well as language to avoid and tips for writing that grabs the reader's attention.

- **Chapter 9, Your Final Draft Checklist, Step 6: Revise and Finalize.** Now that you are equipped with all the tools you need to create a well-written, effective, engaging essay and have worked your way up the ladder one step at a time . . . you're almost at the top. In this chapter you'll learn how to revise your first draft—putting all the steps to use—and write a final draft that showcases both your ideas and your writing skill.

- **Chapter 10, A Final Look, Step 7: Proofread.** You now have a well-thought-out, well-constructed, quality essay, and it's been hard work. There's just one more thing to do before you turn it in—proofread. Any time you are writing where it matters how you and your writing are perceived, proofreading is essential. This chapter—your last step—teaches you quick and easy ways to proofread your work like a professional, giving your essay the polish and finishing touches it needs to be first class.

- **Chapter 11, A Finished Assignment: From Beginning to End.** If you've followed the steps up the ladder we've presented in this book, you're at the top. Congratulations! Here we show you an example of a finished assignment from beginning to end. It takes you through each step, so you can see what we did, how we executed each step, and what we finally produced.

- **Appendixes.** The appendixes give you some extra help in the form of checklists for specific essay situations, such as book reports, standardized test essays, and college application essays (Appendix A); a grammar and usage glossary of terms (Appendix B); useful word lists (Appendix C); further suggested resources for improved writing, grammar, and word usage (Appendix D); tips on proofreading in stages (Appendix E); and before-and-after writing examples (Appendix F).

- **Answer Key.** This section provides you with all the answers to the practice sessions in the book.

For each step and each tool, we'll tell you **What You Need to Know** and **What You Need to Do**, and we'll provide examples and practice exercises, as well as tips and hints, in the form of **Remember, Extra Help**, **Alert**, and **What if . . .** sidebars to help and encourage you along the way.

When you follow the steps in this book, you will have all you need to produce a first-class essay, one that speaks to its audience, has something to say, clearly makes a point, and makes it well. More important, you will have made great strides in learning how to organize your thoughts around a single point and how to express those thoughts clearly and effectively.

Have fun!

1

The Foundation

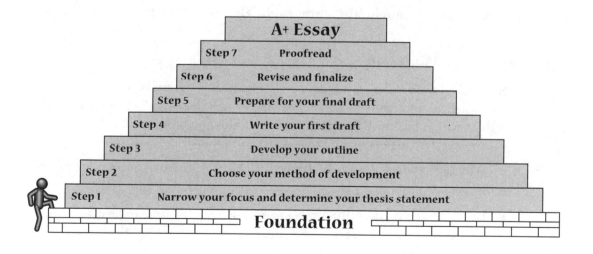

A+ Essay

Step 7	Proofread
Step 6	Revise and finalize
Step 5	Prepare for your final draft
Step 4	Write your first draft
Step 3	Develop your outline
Step 2	Choose your method of development
Step 1	Narrow your focus and determine your thesis statement

Foundation

This book takes you, step-by-step, through the writing process, from generating ideas, through organizing those ideas, and finally to producing a superb finished essay. Throughout the book we will teach you one skill at a time and then build on that skill to move you up the ladder to your goal.

What is the foundation? It's knowing what an essay is, what it aims to do, and how to put it together. When you have a solid foundation to begin the writing process, you build confidence for each of the following steps. Let's start with a stable foundation so your ladder doesn't wobble.

We use the following terms throughout the book:

Prompt. A question or instruction, in the form of a word, sentence, phrase, or idea, that is the subject of your assignment.

Thesis statement. A sentence, usually at the end of your introductory paragraph, that sets up the whole essay; it has a subject and a controlling idea.

Subject. What your paper will be discussing.

Controlling idea. The stance you will be taking on the subject.

Topic sentence. A sentence, usually the first in a developmental paragraph, that presents the point you plan to develop in that paragraph.

Introductory paragraph. The first paragraph in your essay.

Developmental paragraphs. Three to five paragraphs that develop the points of your essay.

Conclusion/concluding paragraph. The last paragraph of the essay.

Reasons for Writing

Let's face it, in most cases, you don't write for yourself—you write for an audience. You need to know what they know and what references and images will appeal to them. Consider the following when establishing who your readers or audience will be:

- Whom do you most want to reach?

- Are they likely to be sympathetic or unsympathetic to your views?

- How are your readers different from you or similar to you in terms of age, education, region, gender, ethnic and cultural heritage, political ideology, and other factors?

- What, if anything, do you want your audience to do as a result of what you write?
- How can you make clear what exactly you want to happen?

What You Need to Know

Essays are written for three major reasons:

- To inform
- To explain
- To persuade

Depending on the result you hope to achieve, you can use various methods of writing—called *methods of development*—which we will cover in the following chapters:

Narration tells a story.
Description presents a picture.
Process tells how to do something or shows how something works.
Comparison/Contrast shows similarities and differences between two or more things.
Cause and Effect examines how one thing leads to another.
Argument/Persuasion aims to convince the readers.

So how do you know which method of development to use for your essay? It depends on your goal.

To Inform

You want to share your knowledge with the readers.

Use Narration (a Story). You have information that you merely want to share with your readers. For example, you might want to tell what happened on your trip to Hawaii or to France. You will need to make a point, such as how wonderful or unusual your experience was.

Use Description. You might want to describe the beach at Waikiki or Parisian architecture so your friend will drool in envy.

To Explain

You want to make a more specific point and help your readers understand what you are discussing. Use one of these three major techniques.

Use Process. In process you want to show readers how easily or effectively they can complete the process or understand why the process works the way it does.

Use Comparison/Contrast. Comparison compares things that are *similar*. Contrast indicates how things are *different*. Generally these are developed in the same essay to show the readers which of the two objects, ideas, or topics is being discussed is better.

Use Cause and Effect. In cause and effect you want your readers to see how one thing caused another and know why this matters.

To Persuade (Sometimes Called Argument)

You want to present a position and convince your readers that it is reasonable and that they should take some action.

Use Argument/Persuasion. The difference between these is that persuasion appeals more to emotion and argument more to logic. Most writers, however, use both.

Parts of an Essay

No matter which method of development you choose, every essay has five parts, each with a specific function in the essay:

The *title* gets the readers' attention and gives a clue as to what the essay will be about.

The *introductory paragraph* grabs the readers' interest and sets up your subject.

The *thesis statement* contains the subject of the essay and the controlling idea (what you plan to say about that subject) and is usually the last sentence in the introductory paragraph.

The *developmental paragraphs* develop the points of your essay. Each starts with a topic sentence that sets up the point to be developed in that paragraph.

The *conclusion* reinforces or summarizes your point in a final paragraph.

What You Need to Do

In order to develop and write a top-notch essay you should include all of the following steps. Depending on the time you have to write—briefly in class or at length at home—some steps may be combined or abbreviated. On some level, however, it's important to complete each of them.

Once you have been assigned or have chosen your prompt—the general subject of your essay—you will:

Step 1: Narrow your focus and determine your thesis statement
Step 2: Choose your method of development
Step 3: Develop your outline
Step 4: Write your first draft
Step 5: Prepare for your final draft
Step 6: Revise and finalize your essay
Step 7: Proofread your essay

Next Steps

Now that you have the foundation for writing an effective essay, we'll begin the steps up the ladder—beginning with "Getting Started."

Getting Started

Step 1: Narrow Your Focus and Determine Your Thesis Statement

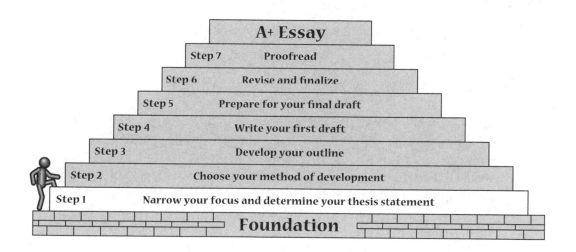

A+ Essay	
Step 7	Proofread
Step 6	Revise and finalize
Step 5	Prepare for your final draft
Step 4	Write your first draft
Step 3	Develop your outline
Step 2	Choose your method of development
Step 1	Narrow your focus and determine your thesis statement
Foundation	

Often, the hardest part of any assignment is getting started. In this chapter, we'll present an example essay, but the approach can apply to any topic. Let's say your assignment is to write an essay of 500 to 650 words on the prompt *Going green is important.* You are to discuss some aspect of improving our environment. You think, "All I know about going green is a song by Kermit the frog." This chapter introduces four tasks that will get you on your way to a successful essay.

Covered in This Chapter

- ☐ **Your first free writing.** Free writing is a method to help you decide what you want to write about.
- ☐ **Research.** Use research to help determine a direction and narrow down your topic.
- ☐ **Your second free writing.** A second free writing helps you determine more of what you know, what interests you, and what you want to write about, focusing on your subject.
- ☐ **Your thesis statement.** A thesis statement is one sentence that sets the foundation on which you will build the whole essay. It usually is the last sentence in your introductory paragraph.

Your First Free Writing

Free writing is a method to help you choose a specific topic for your essay.

 ## What You Need to Know

Actually, you'd be surprised at what you already know. We all have information stored in our subconscious, but we can't always readily access it. For example, say you're trying to remember the name of your fourth-grade art teacher. The harder you try, the farther away it gets. Then you quit trying, wake up the next morning, and think, "Of course. Her name was Ms. Bell." It was in your subconscious all the time, and it just needed to be brought to the surface.

Building on this concept, Peter Elbow, professor and renowned author of several books on writing and writing theory, introduced the idea of free writing. This technique acknowledges the advantage of using the subconscious as an aid to writing. His theory is that if we can cancel out our conscious mind, we will be able to access all the wonderful information we have in our subconscious.

Before you begin to write, however, you can add some tools to the mix to make your free writing more useful. For example, add to your collection of information on your prompt of *Going green is important*:

- You've probably heard things about ecology on TV—and stored it somewhere in the recesses of your mind.

- You can talk to people—classmates, parents, other adults—with information and opinions on the topic.

- You could read articles on "green" online.

Then, armed with both conscious and subconscious information, you have a place to start.

 ## What You Need to Do

The technique of free writing requires you to do only three things:

- Set a timer or alarm.
- Sit down at your computer with no noise.
- Write without stopping.

Set the alarm for 10 minutes. Then start typing. Type anything at all that comes to mind. Keep going, without stopping, until the alarm goes off. Don't worry about grammar or even making sense. The whole idea is to *not* think—just type and see what comes of it.

 Remember

Whatever you do, *don't stop* writing during the 10 minutes—no matter what you write.

 What if...

You can't think of anything to say?
Repeat the last word until words flow again.

Your first free writing on *Going green is important* might look like this (particularly if your automatic spell-check is off).

First Free Writing Example

I don't see why I hve to do a paper on green thins, except for money of course and I guess I also like green grass and I would hate to live where there was no gren grass. I can't make grasss but maybe I might be able to do something to make things better. I know my parents recycle all the garbage and I wonder where all that garbage goes but I'd still be happier if I didn't have to writ ethis dumb paper. Peter, my best friend doesn't have any trouble writing papers. I did like that rticle I read about doing little things that make a difference. But it's the big companies that need to clear up their act Ugh, all of this stuff will need some research. I could even go to the library and hang out with some friends. We always have a good time when I go there there, there, their. Mark has been volunteering for beach cleanup I could talk to him.

Results of First Free Writing

If you have enough time in your schedule, don't read your writing now—wait for a day, or at least a few hours. Then go back and take a look at what you wrote. Ask yourself:

Is there one idea that stands out?
Yes. I kept mentioning doing something to make things better.

Is there something I want to know more about?
Yes. Why bother with recycling? How much good does all this work
   actually do?

Does all that careful recycling actually do some good?
I don't know, and I want to find out. Where does it all go, how is it put
   back to use, and how much difference does it make?

Extra Help

If you don't have time to let your free writing rest, look over your writing and see if you can pull out three points to develop. Or, if you have an in-class essay, stop and think before you write. Then list three points you can cover. The pause gives you time to settle; the three points give you a direction.

Research

The next step in the process is to conduct more research to help you determine your direction.

What You Need to Know

Your first free writing should help you form a focus on what part of *Going green is important* might interest you and what you want to write about. Conducting research will help narrow your focus even more. Following are some items to consider during your research:

- Determine the question you will be answering in your essay.
- Identify the main concepts or keywords in your question.
- Use those keywords to search indexes of encyclopedias and online resources.
- Record the bibliography information for each resource from which you use information.
- Evaluate what you find. If you have too much information, you may need to narrow or even broaden your subject.

What You Need to Do

It's now time to research different aspects of your prompt subject, with the goal of choosing the specific topic for your essay. Some possible topics to explore include:

- What we all can do for our school, neighborhood, or city
- The benefits of recycling
- How we can conserve resources

Once you've identified a topic of interest, you can concentrate on the research. Fortunately you have a wealth of research at your fingertips:

- You have the Internet. You can use your favorite search engine to discover sources of information.

 Alert

If you type in "going green," you'll get more hits than you'll ever need, so you may have to try different keywords to narrow down your search. In selecting articles, we are usually drawn to ones with titles we like. Not always scientific, but fun.

- Check online encyclopedias—but *not* simply Wikipedia, which is not always accurate.

 Alert

Though Wikipedia is a popular online resource, do not consider it a reliable resource, as it is not always accurate. Generally, URLs ending in .edu are more reliable.

- Talk to people you know and respect. For this topic, you could visit a recycling center or a volunteer group actually working at keeping our planet green.
- Don't forget the library. You might already go there to meet friends, but it also contains a wealth of knowledge. Your best friends at the library are the reference librarians. They can often point you in a direction you would never know existed. Never be shy about asking them for help—that's why they are there.

Taking Notes

Note-taking methods vary, and you should choose what is most comfortable and effective for you. The keys are to:

- Get down enough information to help you recall the major points of the research.
- Put the information in a form in which you are most likely to use the research in your essay.

- Label each note with the author's name and the title; the page number(s), or links that the note comes from; a subject heading or theme; and the type of note it is—quotation, paraphrase, summary, your own comment.

Once you have gathered your research information and sources, make a folder on your computer or keep note cards with all the information noted here. This helps organize your material later when you will need a list of these references at the end of your essay.

Give Credit Where It Is Due

Be sure to give credit to outside sources. Using someone else's words without credit is plagiarism and is considered cheating. You don't want to lose all your hard work, which will happen if you plagiarize.

The list of sources is generally provided in the form of a bibliography where you list all of the pertinent source information. There are different forms and amounts of information required for different resources—books, magazines, TV, and so on. Most often they are listed alphabetically by the author's last name. Here are a few examples:

- For a book:
  Piles, Dirth, *Compost from the Bottom Up.* San Francisco: Nature Press, 2010.

- For an encyclopedia or dictionary:
  "environmentalism." *Merriam-Webster's Collegiate Dictionary*, 13th ed. 2003.

- For a magazine or newspaper article:
  Johnson, Anna. "A Legacy of Going Green." *Time* Magazine Dec. 28, 2011.

- For a website or web page:
  Hartman, Jay. "Save Trees by Reading Ebooks." Jan. 19, 2011. www .untreedreads.com.

Check a reference book or style manual to see different accepted styles. An especially good reference is *The Chicago Manual of Style: The Essential Guide for Writers, Editors, and Publishers*, 16th ed., The University of Chicago Press, 2010. Your teacher may provide you with a model to follow as well.

You can also use brief source credits within the text. Proper style for these would be to surround quoted material in quotation marks, followed by parentheses containing the author's last name and the page number of the source that is fully referenced in your bibliography. For example:

> "Homeowners use up to 10 times more toxic chemicals per acre than farmers." (Wray, 25)

 What if . . .

After you've gathered all this information, you feel overwhelmed?

Believe it or not, that's great! It's always better to have too much information than not enough.

Cluster Your Information

Now that you have a mass of information . . . what do you do with it? You use it to help narrow down the focus of your subject—to choose a specific idea for your essay. One way to generate ideas and group them for good organization is to "cluster" them.

One method for clustering your ideas is to sort them in a document, either on paper or on the computer:

- Start by typing the main subject at the top.
- Then type a list of as many ideas as you can think of related to your subject. You may take these ideas from information you already know or information you gather in your research.
- Next, take a look at the items and see which ones seem to go together.
- As you look at the items, you will begin to see patterns. Move similar items into groups and give each group a word or phrase that describes them.
- Finally, look at the groups and see if there is one set that really grabs your attention.

The following clustering example begins with a random list of ideas and questions about cleaning up the environment. Looking at the list, certain patterns emerge. Some of the topics are general in nature and some can be grouped by location—home, school, outdoors, and so on.

In this example, a student might decide that what's most interesting, most attention grabbing for the teacher, and most directly related to the student's life is writing about how each individual can make a difference at home and at school. Therefore, some of the topics in the "general" category and those in the "home" and "school" categories would be most worthwhile to further research and use as key points of the essay.

Unsorted list

Subject: Improving Our Environment
I like green areas
recycling
where does garbage go?
biggest polluters—people, schools, companies, government?
clean beaches
why bother?
use of fertilizing chemicals on farms
turn off water while brushing your teeth
use less gas, so less pollution
use less heat and air conditioning
use only one paper towel to dry hands
buy household cleaning items with fewer hazardous materials
copy and print on both sides of paper
install a low-flow shower head
use solar power for heating and cooling
reuse items like bags and containers when possible

Sorted List

Improving Our Environment
Car: use less gas, so less pollution
General (I can do): reuse items like bags and containers when possible

General (I'm interested): where does garbage go?
General (I'm interested): why bother?
General: biggest polluters—people, schools, companies, government?
General: I like green areas
General: recycling
Home (I can do): use less heat and air conditioning
Home and office: use solar power for heating and cooling
Home and school (I can do): use only one paper towel to dry hands
Home, school, office (I can do): turn off water while brushing your teeth
Home: buy household cleaning items with fewer hazardous materials
Home: install a low-flow shower head
Office or school: copy and print on both sides of paper
Outdoors (I'd like these): clean beaches
Outdoors: use of fertilizing chemicals on farms

Go through this process as many times as you like to help narrow down your areas of interest and choose your specific topic.

Your Second Free Writing

Now it's time to move up the ladder to the next step—your second free writing.

 ## What You Need to Know

You have much more information now and will be able to more clearly see what you know. Conducting a second free writing allows you—consciously and unconsciously—to incorporate:

- What you initially knew
- The research you've gathered
- Facts and impressions you have developed through your research

All of this brings you closer to narrowing your broad subject to a specific topic on which to base your essay.

What You Need to Do

The same techniques apply in your second free writing as in your first free writing, except for a slightly longer time:

- Set the timer or alarm again, this time for 15 minutes.

- Sit down at your computer with no noise.

- Write—*without stopping.*

Again, if possible, when you're finished, let your writing rest for a day or so. This time you'll be amazed at how much your ideas have developed and how much more information-packed your second free writing is, because of the research you did. As you sort through your ideas in the second free writing, the direction of your essay will become clearer.

Second Free Writing Example

I read a lot of stuff about going green but the article that I really liked was the guy came up with some neat ideas about turnign the water off when you brush your teeth. And using one paper towel in the restroom instead of two. And it seems to me that if I keep looking I'll find all kinds of things that I never thought of. and I'm not sure that I want to do all those things. it seems that things are getting so complicated complicated complicated, but I guess doing something is better than doing nohthitng, but diong nothing eseems so much easier but that won't get me anywhere. I've got to figure out what to do. oh, another thing that I read is how much we can make a difference at school in the different ways we do things. that's something I'd definitely be interested in, because there's a lot of waste in schools.

Notice that in this second free writing there is new information, such as "the article that I really liked was the guy came up with some neat ideas about turning the water off when you brush your teeth," and your impressions and interests, such as "I've got to figure out what to do."

Your Thesis Statement

Armed with all the information you've gathered from your research and free writing, you are now ready for the next step—forming a working thesis statement. This will serve as the foundation for your essay.

What You Need to Know

What exactly is a thesis statement? It is one sentence that sets the foundation on which you will build the whole essay. An effective thesis statement includes and accomplishes two things:

- It introduces the *subject*, which signals the reader what you will be writing about.

- It sets the *controlling idea*, the position you will be taking in your paper. It is an idea that needs to be proved or explained.

Extra Help

The thesis statement is usually the last sentence in your introductory paragraph.

What You Need to Do

To write an effective thesis statement, keep the following in mind:

- The thesis statement cannot be a question because then your essay would not develop an idea but would only answer the question.

    Instead of asking, "Why is going green important?" you can change it to, "Going green is important." Now, this statement can and needs to be explained.

- The thesis statement cannot be a fact because a fact does not need to be explained.

    The fact "Recycling saves one million dollars a month" is either true or not, but it does not need to be explained.

Let's say you've chosen to discuss how individuals can help make our planet greener. In your thesis statement, the subject will relate to *making our planet greener,* and the controlling idea is *how we can do that.*

Remember

A good thesis statement always has both the subject and the controlling idea to guide both readers and the writer.

In some cases your teacher may ask you to list the points you are going to cover in the essay in your thesis statement. For example, using the broad theme *Going green is important,* you can be more specific in your topic with "Individuals can help make our planet greener at school, at home, and in our community." In this thesis statement, the readers know exactly what you will discuss in your essay.

Alert

You can take a more subtle approach if you don't want to telegraph the whole essay and want, instead, to keep the readers more in suspense. The danger here is that if you don't list your points up front, you might get off-topic. Of course, use the style your teacher requests.

What if…

After you have finished the paper, or even while you're working on it, you decide that the thesis needs to be changed?

That's perfectly all right. You just need to be sure that your paper and your thesis are in sync and prove what they set out to prove.

Practice Thesis Statements

The better you can identify subjects and controlling ideas in thesis statements, the easier it will be for you to write effective ones. Following are five thesis statements. Underline the subject and write S above it. Then underline the controlling idea and write C over it. See the Answer Key at the end of this book for the correct answers.

1. Recycling can make a real difference.

2. Going green really starts at home.

3. Recycling seems to be a good idea.

4. One person can do a lot to make a difference.

5. More Kermits can make a greener planet.

Next Steps

You've taken the first key steps to creating a successful essay. You've expressed your ideas in free writings, researched your topic, and developed your thesis statement. Now you're ready to take the next step of determining your method of development—*how* you will present your ideas.

3

Methods of Development

Step 2: Choose Your Method of Development

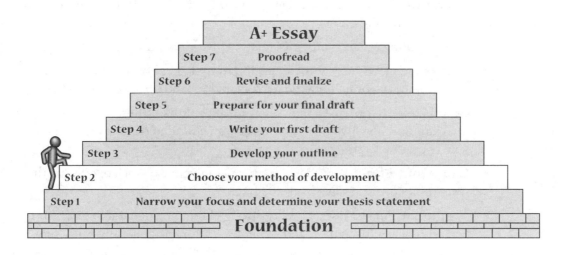

Now that you know how to get started on your essay, choose your topic, and write your thesis statement, you are ready to choose how to develop your idea. Depending on the result you hope to achieve, you can use various methods of writing called *methods of development*. In this chapter, we'll look at some of the more common methods of development. The method of development you choose depends on the ultimate goal for your essay and determines the approach you take in writing your essay.

Covered in This Chapter

- ☐ **Narration.** Tells a story.
- ☐ **Description.** Paints a picture.
- ☐ **Process.** Tells how to do something or understand how something works.
- ☐ **Comparison/contrast.** Shows how alike or unlike things are.
- ☐ **Cause and effect.** Examines how one thing leads to another.
- ☐ **Argument/persuasion.** Aims to convince the reader.
- ☐ **Transitions.** Connect a train of thought.
- ☐ **Fallacies.** Are misleading notions.
- ☐ **Method examples.** Show how each of these approaches works.

Six Methods of Development

- **Narration.** An account of events, most often told in chronological order, to make a specific point.

- **Description.** An account that creates a vivid mental image.

- **Process.** Follows a series of steps, in chronological order, detailing how to do something or helping the readers understand how something works.

- **Comparison/Contrast.** Shows how alike or unlike things are; *comparison* examines how two or more things are *similar*, and *contrast* examines how two or more things are *different*.

- **Cause and Effect.** *Cause* is the reason an event took place; *effect* is the result of an event. Cause leads to effect.

- **Argument/Persuasion.** Makes a strong claim on a debatable topic, supported by facts, examples, and opinions; *argument* generally relies more on logic, while *persuasion* uses more emotion. Most essays contain both.

Remember

The goal of every essay is to make a point and provide insight for the reader. "No insight, no essay."

Every method of development needs to include these elements:

- An understanding of what the particular method requires
- A thesis statement that establishes the topic and your point
- Adherence to the method you've chosen

Remember

Whether the topic and method of development are assigned to you or you choose them, keep in mind what you're trying to accomplish. When you're clear about the direction, purpose, and point of your essay, it is easier to stick to your topic, as well as the format, and you can more effectively present your ideas to your readers.

Let's look at how each of these methods can lead to an effective essay. We'll continue with our "going green" topic and write an introductory paragraph for each method of development. Notice how the essay changes as we alter the thesis statement to fit each method.

Extra Help

An introductory paragraph uses one of these methods:

Asks an intriguing question

Uses a startling fact

Uses a quote

Tells a story

You can read about introductory paragraphs in Chapter 5.

Definition: *Narration is an account of events, most often told in chronological order, to make a specific point.*

Narration

Most people like a good story, but narrative essays go beyond that. They tell a story to make a point, which is generally established as the controlling idea in your thesis statement.

Using our previous thesis statement, "Individuals can help make our planet greener," you might want to tell how you came to that conclusion in a narration essay. You could start with this introductory paragraph that tells a story. Note that the last sentence in this example is your thesis statement.

I'd never taken much notice of recycling and trash in our community. Then I met some people who volunteered in several campaigns to "go green." They talked me into helping with a beach cleanup project. That experience really opened my eyes to what individuals can do to improve our environment.

That's a good beginning and it seems to lead naturally into telling the story of what happened at the beach. It's best to stay in chronological order (time order) so your readers don't get lost; however, just listing the events in order will not necessarily hold the readers' interest. Action and conflict add that interest to your story.

Action gets the readers involved. Rather than:

> We all started picking up the trash on the beach.

Put the readers there:

> As we bent and rose, we looked like waves rising and falling on the beach.

Now the readers have a picture, so they're more engaged in the story. *Conflict* also adds interest. Rather than:

> As we were working, we saw some people leave trash on the beach.

Show your reaction:

> When we saw some people leaving trash on the beach, it bothered us, so we asked them to pick it up, and they put their trash in our bags.

Telling how you feel will make the readers feel more a part of the story, and they will want to know what happens next.

Now you have your readers' attention, and you can go on to tell what happened next and what you learned along the way. Finally, you can close your essay with how you've become involved in cleaning up trash and how you personally have helped make ours a greener planet.

> **Definition:** *A description is an account that creates a vivid mental image.*

Description

Sometimes almost an entire essay can be made up of descriptions. Often descriptions enliven other writing when used as a part of other methods of development. Description can enhance any writing: fiction, history, biography, even technical writing. The purpose is to let the readers see exactly what you are saying. Description will help you drive home your points vividly. The most effective way to show your readers what you're talking about is to use language and images that relate to the five senses (sight, taste, hearing, feel, smell).

For example, if you want to share the horror of what has happened to our planet, you might describe the scene that led you to that conclusion. You could start:

I flew back to Texas to visit some of my cousins. We had played together constantly while growing up, and I was looking forward to some more good times. We'd had so much fun over the years at the old creek and I couldn't wait to feel that cool water again on my back. When I suggested going there, the cousins grinned and, reluctantly, said okay. I couldn't believe how such a beautiful spot had been destroyed.

Now you would vividly describe what you saw, what made it so awful to you, and how that affected you. Your aim is to horrify the readers and show why you've become so involved in green projects.

Your next paragraph, with an opening topic sentence that ties into your thesis statement, might be:

Remembering what used to be made it even worse. Once pecan and oak trees shaded the area. Now I saw only tangled brown bushes, with tufts that looked as if an animal had left its fur there. The buttercups and even the dandelions were gone too. The wind used to sigh through the trees, but no more—no more trees. What used to be grassy banks had become slicky mud, more like oil than ground. I wanted to cry. I asked my cousins "How could this happen?" They only shrugged and took me farther beyond the creek.

You want the readers to be there by your side. Good description lets the readers share your vision. To reinforce the direction of your essay, you might end the essay with this final sentence.

The horror I saw in Texas motivated me to become involved in projects to clean up and prevent this kind of destruction.

The goal is to motivate your readers to get involved also.

> **Definition:** *Process follows a series of steps, in chronological order, to help the readers understand how something works or how to do something.*

Process

We constantly perform processes. Fixing our breakfast, preparing for school or work, and researching online are all processes. Although the basic format for most process essays—often referred to as process papers—is the same, there are slight differences in writing an essay either to *understand how something works* or to *explain or teach how to do something*. Let's take a look at these separately.

Using the thesis statement, "Computers have some special features that make writing easier," we'll present two paragraphs that illustrate the difference.

Understand a Process

The Find and Replace feature in word-processing programs is invaluable in keeping details in a document consistent. As you work, you'll come across details that seem inconsistent—a spelling difference here, a heading style there, a capital letter someplace else—and you'll want to make sure that item is treated the same throughout your document. For example, you might realize that sometimes you used *email*, and sometimes *e-mail*, and you prefer *email*. With the Find and Replace feature, you can search, in seconds, for the tiniest detail in the longest document and then replace any incorrect usage with what you prefer. With this feature, you can just type in what you're looking for and what you'd like to replace it with. You can make the substitution on a case-by-case basis or with a single click of Replace All. This feature also offers several choices of what to look for and how to refine your search. With all of these options, the Find and Replace feature can help ensure accuracy and consistency throughout your document.

Explain a Process

The Find and Replace feature in word-processing programs is invaluable in keeping details in a document consistent. As you work, you'll come across details that seem inconsistent—a spelling difference here, a heading style there, a capital letter someplace else—and you'll want to make sure that item is treated the same throughout your document. With the Find and Replace feature, you can search, in seconds, for the tiniest detail in the longest document and then replace any incorrect usage with what you prefer. For example, you might realize that sometimes you used *email*, and sometimes *e-mail*, and you prefer *email*. Follow this process to make them all consistent as *email*:

- Press Ctrl+H and the Find and Replace dialog box will appear.

- In the Find what: field, type in what you're looking for—in this case, *e-mail*.

- In the Replace with: field, type in what you'd like to replace it with—in this case, *email*.

- To make the substitution on a case-by-case basis, click on the Next button, and when you are taken to each occurrence of *e-mail*, click on the Replace button.

- To change all occurrences of *e-mail* to *email* at once, click on the Replace All button (but be leery of this choice as it may change items you didn't intend to change).

The Find and Replace feature can help ensure accuracy and consistency throughout your document.

Alert

In an essay intended to teach the readers precisely how to perform a process, remember to be complete. Often, when you know something very well, you will leave out steps and, therefore, the process will not work for your readers.

The most important process papers you write will probably be those in a business or work environment, where it is important that a task be performed properly. Learning to write an effective process paper will be valuable throughout your life.

Definition: *Comparison examines how two or more things are similar. Contrast examines how two or more things are different.*

Comparison/Contrast

Teachers assign a comparison/contrast essay for a variety of subjects. You may be comparing the merits of buying a Mac or a PC, which college to attend, two poems, or where to go on vacation. Almost always, you are trying to decide which option better fits your needs or requirements.

Alert

Be careful to compare things that are actually comparable. There is not much to compare between bananas and Facebook.

Often ideas become clearer when they are presented and analyzed based on how they relate to one another. Comparison and contrast allow a writer to explore the ways in which ideas are related. Often, comparison and contrast are used in the same essay.

As an example, a possible introduction and thesis statement might be:

I've become so much more aware of ecology since I first noticed the mounds of garbage outside the mall stores late one night. I checked Google and discovered how much the United States is actually doing to correct the nation's bad habits. The other day, however, I read an article about what Sweden is doing to "be green." We could learn some valuable techniques by looking at what they are doing.

Alert

Be sure that after you've compared and contrasted you've actually made a point. It's not enough to show the differences—you need to let the readers know why it matters to them.

Block and Alternating Methods

There are two primary techniques to use in a comparison/contrast essay—the *block method* and the *alternating method.* As an example, let's compare and contrast two books, *The Old Man and the Sea* and *The Life of Pi*.

What does an 85-year-old Cuban man have in common with a 14-year-old Indian boy? Not much you'd say. But you'd be only half-right. Both of them went through life-changing events. Following Santiago and Pi through their adventures shows us how perseverance can conquer adversity. Though the characters are very different, both books discuss the same thing—how we can conquer our fears.

Using the *block method* in your developmental paragraphs (discussed further in Chapter 5), begin by discussing one book and three key points about that book, for example:

- Age
- The ordeal
- The outcome

In the next paragraph you would do the same for the other book. In the third developmental paragraph, you'd show how these factors impacted the characters.

Alert

With the block method, be careful to cover the same points for each item being compared or contrasted.

The block method forces the readers to keep track of the items in the previous paragraph. For many, a clearer method is the *alternating method*. With this technique, you alternate your information within paragraphs. For example, your first developmental paragraph would discuss how age contributed to Santiago's situation and then Pi's situation, Santiago's ordeal and then Pi's ordeal, and finally the importance of the outcomes. Your conclusion to either method shows what the readers can learn by reading these two books.

> **Definition:** *A cause is the reason an event took place. An effect is the result of an event. Cause leads to effect.*

Cause and Effect

A cause-and-effect essay explains why something happened. *Cause* examines why actions, events, or conditions exist, while *effect* looks at the consequences.

In many situations we question what happened or what to do. *Why did Scott stop dating Jeannie? What will happen if I join a soccer team, on top of my already packed schedule? Will I benefit from getting a part-time job?* By choosing cause and effect as our method of development for discussing the green theme, our introductory paragraph might look like this:

I threw the can in the trash. My mother had taught me to be neat and pick up after myself. But my friend Marsha yelled at me, "What are you doing, don't you know you need to recycle those cans? Why do you want to mess up our planet?" Frankly, I just hadn't thought about it. Since then, I've learned ways I can contribute to making our planet greener and healthier.

Next you discuss what we are doing now to reverse the negative trend of trashing our planet and show what the projected results would be. This takes some research, but the aim is to show how much cleaner our environment will be if we act now.

Alert

Be careful to not attribute an effect to the wrong cause. If a person is failing a course and is always late to class, it's easy to say, "He's always late and that's why he's failing." Actually, he might be failing simply because he doesn't do the work and he is often late because his ride is usually late.

Remember to stay focused on your main point throughout your essay. Ask yourself, why are you telling your readers these facts? You might want to warn them of a danger (increasing garbage is a danger to our planet). Or you might want to show how doing something produces consequences. In the thesis statement mentioned previously, you're telling your readers these facts because you want them to take some action.

> **Definition:** *An argument/persuasion essay makes a strong claim on a debatable topic, supported by facts, examples, and opinions. Argument generally relies more on logic, while persuasion uses more emotion. Most essays contain both.*

Argument/Persuasion

To many people the word *argument* means loud voices, insults, and disharmony. In developing an essay, however, it means constructing logical evidence to convince the readers to accept an opinion, take some action, or do both. Remember, when writing an argument/persuasion essay, presume that the readers do not agree with you. Argument/persuasion as a method of development has three ultimate aims:

- To stir the readers to action
- To change the readers' minds
- To help the readers understand your point of view

Rosie fixed a marvelous meal for us last night: roasted chicken, fresh corn, and green beans. I commented on how tasty everything was. She said, "That's because all the ingredients are organic." She went on to explain not only how organic food tastes better but how going organic is better for our planet. She had some pretty convincing arguments about why buying organic can be so beneficial.

Good arguments rest on a clear, logical foundation (argument); however, logic alone does not generally convince readers. It helps to include some emotional appeal (persuasion) to stir the readers and get them involved. Just as logic benefits from an emotional appeal, an emotional appeal should be substantiated by solid evidence. An argument, then, consists of a conclusion you want to support, your reasons for that conclusion, and the evidence that supports your reasons.

Extra Help

The opinions of authorities add weight to your argument. Use quotes from well-known and acknowledged experts—people and written material—to support your claims.

The first step in developing an argument essay is to find a topic that has two sides, preferably a topic that interests you and one that you can research. Your thesis statement, as always, will signal your direction, but you need to be careful that you do not alienate your readers. Asserting a thesis statement and backing it up with reasons, evidence, and the emotional appeal are key pieces in an argument/persuasion essay, but they are not enough. You need to also acknowledge your readers' possible objections to your point of view—called *counterclaims*—and answer those objections. Otherwise, readers may be less likely to consider your opinion. since they feel you didn't consider theirs.

A thesis statement such as the following won't be very effective, or create interest in what you have to say.

Obviously, everyone should actively recycle.

If something really is obvious, you don't need to argue for it. Also, the word *everyone* is seldom successful. If your readers are not one of everyone, you will alienate them and they won't read on. If your readers don't agree with you, then they may feel you're questioning their intelligence. A better thesis statement could be:

Recycling can be worth the effort.

Even if the readers don't agree, they would probably read on to see what you have to say.

In developing the body of an argument/persuasion essay, you could start each paragraph with a *counterclaim*, such as:

Many people claim it takes too much time to recycle.

To refute this claim, you might counter with:

It doesn't take that much time to recycle if you're well organized.

Your conclusion, then, should reiterate your position in a positive way.

It takes less time than you think to recycle, and the rewards are great for everyone.

Although it takes a little time and some effort, the benefits of learning to argue effectively can be beneficial in clarifying your thoughts. Looking at both sides of an issue can provide more insight and broaden your view of the subject.

If you have been clear, positive, and logical; have appealed to your readers' emotions; and have backed up your opinion with the opinions of authorities, your readers should understand your side, even if they haven't changed their minds.

Extra Help

Although most essays have a clear method of development, they can use elements from other methods. A process paper may use description to make explaining a step more vivid, or a persuasive paper may use a story (narration) to make a point. Remember to primarily stick to the method you've chosen.

Transitions

One device that helps your readers follow a train of thought is the use of transitions. Transitions provide the glue that holds an essay together. They help readers clearly follow what you have to say and consist mainly of the following:

- Connective words and phrases
- Repeated keywords
- Pronouns and demonstrative adjectives
- Parallelism

Without transitions, readers can easily become lost, but be careful not to overuse transitions; you don't need one in every sentence. Use transitions to join complex ideas or to give structure to a long paragraph.

Connective Words and Phrases

Use connective words and phrases to show relationships. Something as simple as *too, then, but, however, on the other hand, yet, because, after, as a result, also, besides, while,* and *next* can move your essay along.

> I like Facebook *because* it gives me a way to make friends around the world. *As a result* of my having a Facebook account, I was invited to visit a friend in France.

Repeated Keywords

To keep the readers on track, it can help to repeat keywords. You have to be careful, though, not to overdo it or you will lose your readers.

> Being intelligent is rewarding. Being popular is fun. Being both is a great combination.

Pronouns and Demonstrative Adjectives

Pronouns stand in for nouns and, so, prevent the monotony of repeating those nouns. Demonstrative adjectives (*this, that, these, those*) also help hook ideas together.

> I always have great *thoughts*, but *these* never seem to be available for an exam.

Parallelism

With pronouns and demonstrative adjectives, you need to be sure the reference is clear and that the replacement agrees in number and gender with the noun.

> If you say, "Paul waited, but when Tommy was late he got upset," it's not clear who is upset.
>
> It is clearer to say "Paul waited, but he got upset when Tommy was late."

Fallacies

A major danger in writing (and thinking) occurs when you fall prey to what are termed *logical fallacies*. There are eight commonly accepted logical fallacies:

- **Hasty Generalization.** Drawing a conclusion from too little evidence. (*The teenagers I work with do as little as possible, so I know that young people aren't hard workers.*)

- **Stereotyping.** Attaching supposed characteristics to a group. (*Surfers are all irresponsible.*)

- **Either/Or.** Assertions that only two options exist. (*Either you buy a car or you can't go to the school across town.*)

- **Begging the Question.** Arguing that a claim is true by repeating that claim in other words. (*You should drive 65 miles per hour on the freeway because that is what the law says, and the law is the law.*)

- **Ad Hominem.** Attacking the person rather than the position. (*Dianne's new business idea will never work because she never got a college degree.*)

- **Post Hoc, Ergo Propter Hoc.** Claiming that one thing caused another thing when there may be no connection. (*I fell asleep doing my homework, so homework makes people sleepy.*)

- **Faulty Analogy.** Assuming that if one thing resembles another, conclusions made on one apply to the other. (*Well, the plane model worked in the wind tunnel, so that plane will fly.*)

- **Slippery Slope.** Pretending that one thing inevitably leads to another. (*We can't reduce our military budget. The whole world will think we are a weak country.*)

It's important to avoid these fallacies, since they considerably weaken your effectiveness.

Method Examples

Choosing your method of development allows you to more clearly see your goal: a well-written, first-class essay. Your method also helps you shape your thesis statement. Following are examples of how one fact can be used to create different thesis statements depending on the direction you want your essay to take.

We'll start with a fact (which cannot be a thesis statement because there is no controlling idea). Then, you'll see how, with a little tweaking, you can create an appropriate thesis statement for each method of development.

Fact: I went to Disneyland last weekend.

- **Narration.** Tell the story of what happened and how it was unexpected.

We had an unexpected adventure when we went to Disneyland.

- **Description.** Pick three sights and show how they were unexpected.

  Disneyland presents so many unexpected sights.

- **Comparison/Contrast.** Pick three things and show how they were and how they have changed, and why that matters to you.

  Disneyland has certainly changed since I first went there five years ago.

- **Cause and Effect.** Tell how Disneyland's methods have caused these changes.

  Disneyland has changed the way most theme parks operate.

- **Process.** Show what you need to do.

  With a little careful planning, you can make your trip to Disneyland successful.

- **Argument/Persuasion.** Be aware and mention why some think the trip is *not* beneficial and then show how these objections might be incorrect.

  Although some may not agree, the cost of a trip to Disneyland can be well worth it.

Practice Methods of Development

To check how well you can identify the various methods of development, identify which type of essay each of these thesis statements sets up (*narration, description, process, comparison/contrast, cause and effect,* or *argument/persuasion*), and underline the key word(s) in each that lead(s) to your decision. See the Answer Key at the end of this book for the correct answers.

1. It's difficult to decide which type of exercise program is best.

2. Schools should do more to develop students' physical development.

3. I will always remember the sights and sounds of my first baseball game.

4. Exercising can change your life in more ways than one.

5. By learning these simple steps, you too can develop an effective exercise program.

6. I discovered that playing sports involves more than skill.

Next Steps

As you can see, the goal of your essay influences which method of development you use. The deciding factors remain—what do you want to achieve and how can you best do so? Appendix A: Checklists for Specific Essay Types will help you not only with the methods of development described here but also with essays that focus on particular themes, including book reports, standardized test essays, and college application essays. Once you've decided which method fits your needs, you're ready to take the next step—creating an outline for your essay.

Form a Plan: Outlines

Step 3: Develop Your Outline

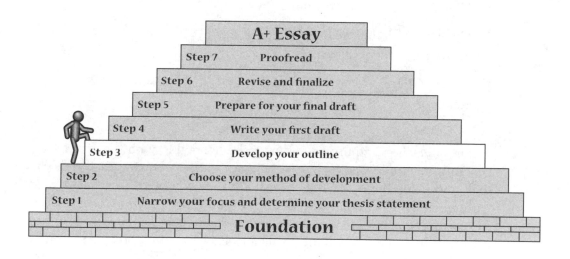

A+ Essay

Step 7	Proofread
Step 6	Revise and finalize
Step 5	Prepare for your final draft
Step 4	Write your first draft
Step 3	Develop your outline
Step 2	Choose your method of development
Step 1	Narrow your focus and determine your thesis statement

Foundation

Once you have chosen a topic and method of development for an essay, you're ready to write, right? Not quite yet. You need a plan—an outline—so you can present your ideas clearly and coherently. This chapter discusses all three outline forms and how they help bring your ideas together to create the first draft of your essay.

Covered in This Chapter

☐ **Formal topic outline.** Uses key words or phrases to list the progression of your essay.

☐ **Sentence outline.** Lists the key points and the topic sentences for the developmental paragraphs of your essay.

☐ **1-2-3 outline.** Includes the thesis statement and three key points to discuss.

☐ **In-class essay exam.** Uses an abbreviated 1-2-3 process to organize your answers.

What You Need to Know

An outline indicates your plan for showing:

- Your thesis statement
- The three main points of your essay
- The details supporting those points

There are three types of outlines:

- Formal topic
- Sentence
- 1-2-3

Often teachers require an outline to be handed in with the essay. They generally want a formal topic or a sentence outline showing each step you took to develop the essay. But, even if not required by the teacher, a good outline will keep you on track and make the whole writing process easier. Also, learning to outline your ideas, whether for a paper, for a talk, or just to get your ideas in order, will be a valuable asset both in school and in other areas of your life.

What You Need to Do

At first, developing an outline may be somewhat difficult, but the process becomes easier the more you do it. Sorting out your ideas and then re-sorting them and organizing them into the most effective format takes time and thought.

Once you have completed your free writing, conducted your research, and determined the approach (method of development) for your essay, use the clustering technique discussed in Chapter 2 to go through your notes and see how ideas cluster. Then, do it again. This will help you discover the main idea you want to discuss, which then becomes your thesis statement.

Next you can group your supporting information under the following major outline divisions. Remember, your thesis statement is always the key starting place for your essay—and your outline.

Extra Help

The most common way to organize details in an essay is chronological order, but other ways to consider are:

- **Order of importance.** Either from least important details leading to most important or most important details to less important. The latter has greater impact.
- **Cause and effect.** Describing the cause of a problem and the effects that resulted from the problem.
- **Order of location.** Arranging details in the order in which you encounter them, such as describing the paintings in a room in a museum from left to right.

Formal Topic Outline

A formal topic outline uses keywords or phrases to list the progression of your essay. Formal topic outlines are rarely used for a writer's own purposes, but since they often are requested by teachers, it's worthwhile to know what they are and how they should be presented.

A standard formal topic outline takes this form:

    I. Introduction
   II. 1st Point
       A. Supporting details for 1st point
          1. Supporting details for A
             a. Supporting detail for A.1
             b. Supporting detail for A.1

    2. Further supporting details for A
       a. Supporting detail for A.2
       b. Supporting detail for A.2
    3. Further supporting details for A
   B. Further supporting details for 1st point
III. 2nd Point

The most important items you are covering in your paper are those at the far left of your outline. In the previous example, these would be the Introduction, 1st Point, 2nd Point, and so on.

Alert

For each 1 you need a 2, and for each A you need a B. If there is only one item, there's no need to make a numbered or lettered entry—as in II.A.3. in our formal topic outline example (no a. or b. needed, because only one point is made).

Let's take a look at an actual formal topic outline. Say the prompt given by the teacher is "Should physical education be mandatory in school?" Your thesis statement might be "PE should be mandatory in school," which would be stated at the end of your introductory paragraph. A portion of your formal topic outline would look like this:

  I. Introduction
 II. Mental benefits of PE
   A. Rests mind
    1. Opens mind
       a. Absorbs more
       b. Retains more
    2. Brings relief
       a. Rests
       b. Time to understand
   B. Future benefits

This outline would certainly be sufficient, but you would still have to come up with topic sentences and more information.

Sentence Outline

A more complete outline, and often a more useful one, is the sentence outline. Creating it takes a little longer, but when you're finished, it almost writes the paper for you—almost.

Here is an example of a sentence outline, using the same thesis statement as earlier, "PE should be mandatory in school."

I. Introduction
II. PE offers some real benefits beyond exercise.
   A. Taking a break can clear the mind.
      1. A rested mind can absorb more.
      2. A rested mind can also retain more.
   B. Exercising the body brings relief to the whole system.
      1. Exercise helps renew attention.
      2. Exercise gives time to understand.
III. PE offers benefits in the future also.

Notice that in the formal topic outline, there are no periods, because the items are not sentences. The sentences in your sentence outline are the topic sentences for the paragraphs of your essay. (See Chapter 5 for more on topic sentences.)

 Extra Help

A topic sentence, usually the first sentence in each developmental paragraph, has the same structure as the thesis statement. It requires a subject and a controlling idea, which you will develop in that paragraph. So, the thesis statement gives the subject and controlling idea for the whole essay, while the topic sentence gives the subject and controlling idea for each developmental paragraph.

1-2-3 Outline

Often, a formal topic or sentence outline is not appropriate for your needs. Three situations where a formal topic or sentence outline might not be needed are:

- An outline is not required.
- You have to write an essay in class or under exam conditions.
- You feel you know what you want to say and don't need an outline.

Even in these situations, you still need some kind of plan to organize your thoughts. This is where an informal outline, called the 1-2-3 outline, can be your best choice. The process of building the 1-2-3 outline is invaluable for both in-class essays and those you do outside of class, and it will give you the foundation for your first draft.

In-Class Essays

These can be daunting. You haven't had time to think about the subject and you may feel you don't even know what you do, in fact, know. Remember, everyone else is in the same place. The worst thing you can do is start writing immediately. Take a few minutes to go over the ideas in your mind. Then see if you can come up with three things to discuss in your essay. Write them down. That's important; you think you'll remember, but actually seeing those ideas will keep you on track. With those three ideas, you've just developed an abbreviated 1-2-3 outline, and it will give you the direction for what you want to say.

Let's look at our PE question, "Should PE be mandatory in school?" You decide the answer is that it should be mandatory in school. You could write down your thesis statement, "PE can be very beneficial to most students" and these three points:

1. Relax mind
2. Relax body
3. Future benefits

Now you're ready to write a coherent essay because you know where you're going.

At-Home Essays

When your essay is a homework assignment (rather than an in-class assignment) you have more time to carefully develop and write your essay, but usually not as much time as you want. This is where the 1-2-3 process can help you make the best use of your time.

Start with your thesis statement and think of three things that will prove your assertion. Then, list the topic sentences you will use to develop each idea. Often that can be enough to get you started. You can go a step further, and list the three points you want to make in each paragraph. You'll wind up with something like this:

PE can be beneficial for most students. (thesis statement)

PE has certain physical benefits. (topic sentence for 1st developmental paragraph)

PE also has mental benefits. (topic sentence for 2nd developmental paragraph)

PE, moreover, has future benefits. (topic sentence for 3rd developmental paragraph)

In-Class Essay Exam

It is important to realize that an essay exam is *not* an essay. In an essay exam you are required to answer a question. Answer the question in the first sentence and list the three points you will use to develop your answer. When you answer the question in the first sentence, the teacher sees that you know the answer. In the rest of the answer, you develop the three points you've listed, and you're almost through. A final sentence ends the answer. Whether your answer needs to be one paragraph or several, the format would be the same.

 What if . . .

Instead of presenting you with a question the teacher tells you to discuss a topic, such as "Discuss the symbolism in Hemingway's 'Hills Like White Elephants'?"

Turn the topic/prompt into a question: "How does Hemingway use symbolism in this story?" Your first sentence might be:

Hemingway uses symbolism in "Hills Like White Elephants" to show the state of the world, the problem for the man, and the problem for the woman.

Now you have a clear structure to write a clear answer.

Practice Outlines

Now that you've learned how to start with an outline and develop an essay—or a paragraph—let's practice creating a brief 1-2-3 outline. Read the narration paragraph here and fill in the blanks in the outline template that follows. See the Answer Key at the end of this book for one possible result.

> I'll always remember Amsterdam. My Mom and I spent three days in Amsterdam and did most of the tourist things. We visited the Van Gogh Museum and were quite impressed. We stopped at shops and headed to the Anne Frank House. Seeing that was a remarkable experience. But what happened next was more memorable. As we walked, my Mom tripped and fell into the canal. And she doesn't swim. Fortunately, I do. I jumped in, grabbed her by the shoulders, and swam her back to the wall, where several people helped us out of the water. Mom said she was very, very glad I had been there to save her life.

I. (topic sentence) _____

   A. (1st point) _____

   B. (2nd point) _____

   C. (3rd point) _____

II. (conclusion) _____

Next Steps

Now that you have learned how to create an effective outline, let's start using it to actually write an essay. The next step is your first draft.

Craft Your First Draft

Step 4: Write Your First Draft

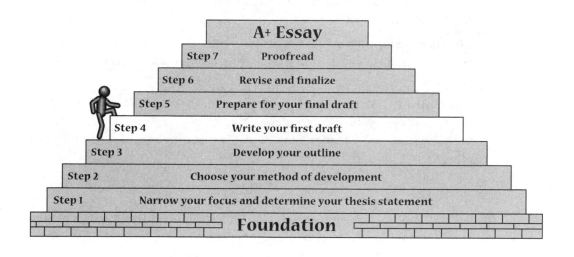

	A+ Essay	
Step 7	Proofread	
Step 6	Revise and finalize	
Step 5	Prepare for your final draft	
Step 4	Write your first draft	
Step 3	Develop your outline	
Step 2	Choose your method of development	
Step 1	Narrow your focus and determine your thesis statement	
	Foundation	

If you've followed the previous steps in this book, you know how to choose a topic to discuss, decide on the method of development for your essay, and develop an outline. Next comes the fun part—writing your first draft. In this chapter you'll learn to effectively develop each key element of your essay.

Covered in This Chapter

- ☐ **Title.** Here is the first chance to grab your readers' attention.
- ☐ **Introductory paragraph.** This paragraph introduces your topic, sets the tone for the essay, and ends with your thesis statement.
- ☐ **Developmental paragraphs.** These paragraphs in the body of your essay lay out and support your key points and begin with a clear topic sentence that conveys the idea of its paragraph.
- ☐ **Concluding paragraph.** This paragraph ends the essay with your ultimate goal achieved or question answered.

What You Need to Know

The standard essay assigned in many classes is generally five paragraphs (approximately 500 words) long and consists of these elements:

- **Title.** Designed to capture the readers' attention

- **Introductory paragraph.** Three to five sentences ending in a clear thesis statement

- **Three developmental paragraphs.** Each with a clear topic sentence and three points, with two to three sentences per point and a concluding sentence

- **Concluding paragraph.** Two to three sentences wrapping up your ideas, restating your thesis statement in a new way, giving a brief summary, leaving your readers something to think about, or calling your readers to an action

Alert

The number of sentences noted in the previous list for developmental paragraphs may seem like a lot. It's perfectly acceptable to make your point effectively with fewer sentences, as long as you have no minimum word count requirement. However, most essays assigned in class do have a required minimum word count—and the teachers do count the words. Using the formula shown will usually bring you to the 500–1,000 word count.

What You Need to Do

Now the fun part. Since you will be rewriting this essay in a final draft later, for this first draft you can write quickly and not worry about how smooth or how complete your paper is. The important thing is to get your ideas down so you can see them and, later, improve on them. Once you have done this, you will be much more relaxed and not as nervous about the assignment, since you've already got some ideas.

In this chapter, we're going to build a first draft, using the 1-2-3 process. We'll continue with the topic of whether PE should be mandatory or is valuable in school, using the thesis statement and three points we established in the previous chapter:

> PE can be beneficial for most students.
> - Physical
> - Mental
> - Future

Since we're advocating action or trying to change our readers' minds, this will be an argument/persuasion essay.

Title

Titles matter. Readers see them first, and they often buy a book or read an article—print or electronic—if the title catches their attention.

What You Need to Know

Publishers have teams of people working weeks, sometimes months, to come up with the best title for a book. That's great for them, but you won't have that kind of time, nor are you trying to sell a book to millions of readers. So don't worry about finding the perfect title. Do give it a fair amount of thought, though, so you choose a title that captures both your readers' attention and the essence of what your essay is about.

What You Need to Do

To produce a good title:

- **Find the common theme in the essay.** If you write an essay about Hawaii, but the main focus of the essay is surfing in Hawaii, then "Surf Hawaii" would be an appropriate name.

- **Keep the title succinct.** You have about three seconds to capture the readers' attention, so a title of two to five words is ideal.

- **Keep the title relevant.** The title should accurately reflect what the paper is about.

- **Choose a title that fits the tone of your paper.** If it's a humorous essay, then a light and funny title would be a good choice.

- **Do not give away too much or the readers may not read on.** "Floating in Hawaii" is more intriguing than "What I Learned on My Trip to Hawaii."

- **Avoid being too general.** "There Is a Lot to See at the Mall" is too broad. Better would be, "The Surprising Mall."

Extra Help

The title stands alone. Do not use it to start the essay. And consider writing your title last, after you've fully developed your essay and what you want to say.

Introductory Paragraph

The introductory paragraph is generally three to five sentences. It lays the foundation for the developmental and concluding paragraphs that follow.

What You Need to Know

Similar to the goal of a good title, your introductory paragraph needs to grab readers' attention so they will want to read on. And though you know your teacher will read on, an effective introductory paragraph will engage both your teacher and an audience, and your readers will tend to be more open to what you have to say in the rest of the essay.

Extra Help

Like the title, some people write their introductory paragraph (or the introduction to a book) last, but you'll need at least a working thesis statement to give direction to your essay.

What You Need to Do

If you begin an essay with, "In this paper I am going to write about . . .," you've already bored your readers and they won't want to go on. In this example, to get the readers on our side, we'll start the introductory paragraph with a story that many readers will identify with, a story that is suited to our purpose and our audience. We end with a strong thesis statement.

> **Story:** I went to PE today, but I really didn't want to. First, it was basketball practice day—and to be honest, I'm not very good at basketball. Also, the last PE period, my friends played a joke on me in the locker room. I talked to my parents about getting out of PE. During our discussion, they pointed out several reasons why PE is really worthwhile.
>
> **Thesis:** Now I realize how students can benefit from taking PE classes.

Note that in the last sentence, which is the thesis statement, "students" is the *subject* and "can benefit" is the *controlling idea*.

Here are four valuable techniques you can use to grab your readers' attention in your introductory paragraph and encourage them to read on:

- Ask an intriguing question.
- Use a startling fact.
- Use a quote.
- Tell a story.

Introductory Paragraph Examples

Let's return to our environmental theme. In the following examples, the last sentence is the thesis statement. You'll note that the wording is slightly altered to fit the particular introductory paragraph, but each retains the initial concept of our thesis statement, "Individuals can help make our planet greener."

1. **Ask an intriguing question.** If you ask "Do you want to have enough food to eat?" the answer is obvious. Who doesn't want to have enough food to eat? Better to ask, "With the terrible state of our planet, should people quit having children?" That seems like a drastic statement, and proposal, but it will certainly grab almost any reader's attention. You might continue:

   > With the terrible state of our planet, should people quit having children? That seems pretty drastic. Yet, at the rate we're using up our natural resources and trashing our planet, some people see this as the ultimate solution to save resources. If we, as individuals, work to make our planet greener, such drastic steps won't be necessary.

2. **Use a startling fact.** "Each person produces about 4.3 pounds of trash each day. That's 200 million tons of trash in the entire United States per day." That image is sure to grab your readers' attention:

   > Each person produces about 4.3 pounds of trash each day. That's 200 million tons of trash in the entire United States per day. Have you ever seen the pile of garbage outside a local fast-food restaurant at night? Did you ever wonder where it all goes? The reality is that it goes to a "landfill," but what exactly does that mean? What will happen when the landfill fills up? We each need to find methods to produce less garbage rather than find more places to put it.

3. **Use a quote.** Quoting an authority shows the importance of your concept, and the readers will usually want to know the significance that quote has both for you and for them.

   > Stuart Udall, former Secretary of the Interior, said, "A land ethic should stress the oneness of our resources and the live-and-help-live logic of the great chain of life." There have been many bills passed to preserve our planet, but without our help, few of them will make a difference. If we become aware of what needs to be done, and take the time to work at conservation, each one of us can make a huge difference.

4. **Tell a story.** Telling a story is often the best way to capture the readers' attention because the audience is intrigued and will want to know what happens.

> Splat! The Taco Shack bag hit my windshield. Fortunately it slipped off so I could see and didn't have an accident. I knew garbage was really bad for the environment, but I didn't realize how bad until it almost hit me in the face. I decided to learn more about what we could do to start eliminating it and cleaning it up.

With each of these introductory paragraphs, you've now successfully signaled to your reader what you will be writing about—the importance of individuals helping to make our planet greener, and cleaner. And you've offered examples of what you think people should do, and how individuals can help—through conservation and prevention.

Developmental Paragraphs

Following the introductory paragraph that ends with the thesis statement are the *body* or *developmental* paragraphs—three paragraphs that will elaborate on the three points you've chosen to discuss.

 ## What You Need to Know

You develop the weight of your essay in these developmental paragraphs. To add details to your ideas, each paragraph sets up one topic and then develops it. Each paragraph for a standard class essay of 500 to 1,000 words should be 10 to 12 sentences long, including:

- A topic sentence
- Two to three sentences supporting each of your three points
- A concluding sentence

The topic sentence starts a paragraph and, like the thesis statement, contains a subject and a controlling idea. The thesis statement sets up the whole essay; a topic sentence sets up a paragraph.

Alert

While the topic sentence is often the first or second one, this is not always the case. A topic sentence can also come at the end of a paragraph, acting as a summary.

What You Need to Do

Each developmental paragraph is like a short essay in its development and goal. You can use the 1-2-3 process for each paragraph—the first sentence introduces your topic, and then you cover the three points you plan to discuss. An outline for a paragraph looks like this:

Topic sentence
    Developmental point 1
        Supporting details (2–3 sentences)
    Developmental point 2
        Supporting details (2–3 sentences)
    Developmental point 3
        Supporting details (2–3 sentences)
Concluding sentence

Using the 1-2-3 process for a standard 500-word essay, here's an example of a first developmental paragraph supporting the point "The mental benefits of PE in school."

Topic sentence: I now know that PE provides positive mental benefits. *Point 1:* Critics say that when students take time out for PE, it detracts from their studies. *Supporting details:* However, research shows that this is not so. (*You would plug in some research here to support this point.*) When students concentrate too much on a subject, their minds almost freeze. *Point 2:* They need to back off and let the information rest for a while. *Supporting details:* If they go from one class to another without a break, ideas become jumbled. When they get back to class, after PE, their minds are clearer and ready for more information. *Point 3:* Another benefit is that a rested mind learns more. *Supporting details:* When a person tries too hard to grasp an idea, such as adding negative numbers, the information doesn't sink in. A mental rest gives the mind time to retain the information before more is added. *Concluding sentence:* PE may seem to take time off from learning, but it actually provides time to let the mind absorb and better understand the material from class.

The 1-2-3 pattern works for all developmental paragraphs. In some instances, you may need four or five sentences to develop a point, but sticking to the three points keeps you on track.

Concluding Paragraph

Use this short paragraph to pull together all your ideas, leave your readers feeling satisfied, and move them to continue thinking about your writing. If you have a short essay, summarizing is not necessary. For the PE paper, we might say:

> Although at first PE may seem a waste of time, when we examine the benefits we find that those benefits far outweigh any detriments. We want students who are alert and productive. The ancient Greeks praised a sound mind in a sound body. PE helps students achieve this ideal.

Alert

Be careful not to merely repeat the thesis statement in your concluding paragraph. Rephrasing it usually works well. This conclusion can be a summary, a restatement of your ideas, an opinion, or a call to action.

Practice Topic Sentences

As you've learned in this chapter, a topic sentence sets the tone for each developmental paragraph. Following are three thesis statements, with a brief 1-2-3 outline for each. Using these as clues to what each developmental paragraph will be about, write a topic sentence for each outline point you might use in your developmental paragraph to support the thesis statement. See the Answer Key at the end of this book for possible results.

Thesis statement 1: Superhero movies have a power of popularity that has lasted nearly since the beginning of film.
   A. Original *Superman* movie, 1978, big box-office hit
   B. *Batman* movies, 1943–2008, consistency in sales
   C. *Iron Man 2*, 2010, more box-office success

Thesis statement 2: While there are some major differences between the *Harry Potter* and *Twilight* series, one of the most important contributions they both have achieved is to encourage young adults to read.
   A. *Harry Potter*, children and adults, wizardry
   B. *Twilight*, tweeners, vampire romance
   C. *Harry Potter* and *Twilight*, new generations of readers, technology generation

Thesis statement 3: It is a common practice in the United States to go directly from high school to college; however, all students should be encouraged to take a year off before enrolling in college.
   A. Travel, nonbook learning, personal growth
   B. Work, privilege of attending college, value of a dollar
   C. Volunteer work, new perspectives, future planning

Next Steps

You've come a long way with your thoughts and your writing. Wasn't it easier using the 1-2-3 process? You're not through yet. If you want to turn this effort into an A paper, you'll need to do some refining and rewriting. The following three chapters will equip you with the tools to make your first draft into a first-class essay.

6

Your Writer's Toolbox: Sentences

Step 5: Prepare for Your Final Draft, Part 1

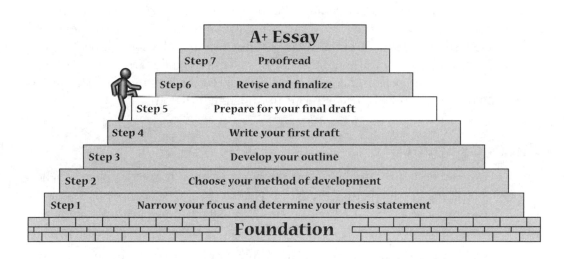

		A+ Essay
	Step 7	Proofread
	Step 6	Revise and finalize
	Step 5	Prepare for your final draft
	Step 4	Write your first draft
	Step 3	Develop your outline
	Step 2	Choose your method of development
	Step 1	Narrow your focus and determine your thesis statement
		Foundation

Once you have the first draft of your essay, the next step is to fine-tune what you've written to create your final essay. This and the following two chapters will be Your Writer's Toolbox—important information about sentences, the mechanics of language, and the style of writing. Review these chapters in advance of sitting down to prepare your final draft.

Covered in This Chapter

- ☐ **Parts of speech.** Learn these pieces of the language puzzle.
- ☐ **Simple sentences.** These are the most basic types of sentences, with one subject and one verb.
- ☐ **Complex sentences.** These contain both a dependent clause and an independent clause (a clause that can stand alone).
- ☐ **Compound sentences.** These contain two independent clauses separated by a semicolon or a word from a list called "FANBOYS," which are those conjunctions that can separate two complete clauses.
- ☐ **Compound/complex sentences.** These are a combination of compound and complex structures, with one dependent clause and two independent clauses.
- ☐ **Key problem areas.** Run-on sentences, comma splices, and fragments cause problems in otherwise clear writing.
- ☐ **Parallel phrasing.** Use similar word patterns for similar ideas.

Part of that process of refining your first draft is to examine each word, sentence, and paragraph to ensure what you've written is correct, clear, and concise. The most essential tools you use to build the paragraphs of your essay are well-crafted sentences. In this chapter you'll learn how to develop effective sentences and how to avoid possible errors. You may find the Grammar and Usage Glossary of Terms in Appendix B helpful.

Parts of Speech

A sentence is like a puzzle, and the parts of speech are the pieces. When the pieces fit, the picture they form is clear. Sentences can be as simple or as expressive as the situation dictates. No matter the length or type of sentence, most of the words you use will be one of these seven parts of speech:

- **Noun.** Indicates a person, place, thing, or idea. A noun can be either plural or singular, and masculine, feminine, or neuter. Proper nouns (*Lois*) start with a capital letter and, unless they begin a sentence, common nouns (*computer, music*) do not.

- **Pronoun.** Takes the place of a noun. Pronouns (*I, he, she, it, them, who that, which, all*) need to agree with the number and gender of the nouns they replace. (*Boomer* ate fast, because *he* was so hungry.)

- **Adjective.** Describes a noun. Adjectives usually go right before the noun (*happy* dog, *fluffy* cat, *radical* idea).

- **Verb.** Describes the action (*run, play*) or state of being of the noun or pronoun (*be, feel, become*). Verbs have tenses, including past, present, and future (*ran, runs, will run*). They need to agree with the subject—who or what is doing the action. (*John is* a soccer star; *Larry and Carl are* soccer stars.)

- **Adverb.** Describes a verb, another adverb, or an adjective. Adverbs add missing specifics (she learns *quickly*; she learns *very* quickly; an *extremely* intelligent child).

- **Preposition.** "Positions" other words in a sentence. Prepositions (*about, above, between, in, on*) show the relationship between nouns (*above* the clouds, *between* two people).

- **Conjunction.** Connects other words, parts of a sentence, or one idea to another. Conjunctions (*and, or, but, because*) join elements (I like both rap *and* rock music; I want an iPad, *but* I can't afford one).

For a complete discussion of these parts of speech, a good handbook to consult is *Easy Grammar Step-by-Step* (McGraw-Hill, 2011).

 Extra Help

To set some words apart and make them special, use capital letters. The major uses of capitals are:

- To mark the first word in a sentence
- For proper nouns (names of a specific person, place, or thing)
- For *I*
- In titles (capitalize the first word and all important words but not prepositions or conjunctions)
- For countries and languages

Sentences

Now let's learn more about the basic building blocks of your writing—sentences. In fact, this is where the real writing begins. By real writing we mean more than just stating facts or opinions; real writing is *how* you state your facts and opinions.

What You Need to Know

There are four types of sentences: simple, complex, compound, and compound/complex. When you use a variety of types, your essay will be stronger, and so will your overall writing. A sentence may express emotions, give orders, make statements, or ask a question. Every sentence must express a complete thought, and it must contain at least one subject-verb combination.

Sentences have two parts:

- The *subject*, which is a noun or pronoun, commonly indicates what the sentence is about or who or what performs the action in the sentence. (*Joe* bought new shoes.)

- The *predicate*, which contains one or more verbs, tells something about the subject and serves to make an assertion or denial about the subject of the sentence. (Karen *is always helping people*.)

What You Need to Do

To make your essays more interesting, use a mixture of sentence types to vary your sentence structure and length. If you use only one type of sentence, your writing, generally, becomes boring.

Simple Sentences. The most basic type of sentence, simple sentences have only one subject and one verb.

> Butterflies flit.
>
> Horses eat.

These sentences offer only the most basic information. But you can do a lot with the basics. Start with a simple sentence, but add prepositional phrases, adjectives, and so on to expand the sentence and give it more meaning.

The bright orange-and-black Monarch butterflies energetically flit about.

This is still a simple sentence with one subject (*butterflies*) and one verb (*flit*), but we've made it much more descriptive. The subject-verb combination will be the heart of each sentence you write, but, remember, to be a sentence, it must contain a complete thought.

Simple sentences, such as the ones shown previously, have one subject and one verb. The subject and verb may be plural, but the sentence is still simple:

Ann and Pat (*subjects*) played (*verb*) Scrabble and ate (*verb*) dinner.

Complex Sentences. These contain a *dependent clause* (a phrase that cannot stand alone) and an *independent clause* (a clause that can stand alone).

When Ann and Pat played Scrabble (*dependent clause*), Pat usually won (*independent clause*).

Compound Sentences. These contain two independent clauses, separated by a semicolon or a word from a list called "FANBOYS," which are those conjunctions that can separate two complete clauses. FANBOYS stands for:

For
And
Nor
But
Or
Yet
So

Ann and Pat play Scrabble every day (*independent clause*), but (*a FANBOYS*) they never get bored (*independent clause*).

Compound/Complex Sentences. These are just what you'd expect—a combination of compound and complex structures with one dependent clause and two independent clauses.

> When I got home last night (*dependent clause*), my mother was waiting up for me (*independent clause*); she was really upset (*independent clause*).

Alert

Subjects and verbs need to agree. If the noun is singular, the verb must be singular too.

> *John*, one of my friends, *works* at Safeway.

John is the singular subject, so we need the singular verb *works* to agree.

> *John and his friends work* there.

You are now dealing with a plural subject (*John and his friends*) and so need the plural verb *work*.

Key Problem Areas

The most common problems that arise while writing sentences are:

- Run-on sentences
- Comma splices
- Fragments

Once you recognize these missteps, you'll be able to fix them.

A *run-on sentence* has two complete thoughts improperly joined:

> I went to the movie last night I really enjoyed it.

To correct, use a FANBOYS or a semicolon between the two complete thoughts, or change to two complete sentences:

> I went to the movie last night, *and* I really enjoyed it.
>
> I went to the movie last night; I really enjoyed it.
>
> I went to the movie last night. I really enjoyed it.

A *comma splice*, like a run-on sentence, has two complete thoughts improperly joined but this time by a comma.

> I texted Jerry, he couldn't answer because he was in class.

To correct, you can change the comma to a semicolon, or add a FANBOYS:

> I texted Jerry, *but* he couldn't answer because he was in class.

A *fragment*, on the other hand, is an incomplete thought and can really confuse your readers.

> Although I am always on time with my assignments for English class.

So? This can be fixed by removing the qualifying word *although* for a complete sentence:

> I am always on time with my assignments for English class. (Note that eliminating "although" can change your intended meaning.)

Or you can change the period to a comma and add a complete thought to form a complete sentence:

> Although I am always on time with my assignments for English class, yesterday I was late.

Following are some hints to help you discover and correct run-on sentences, comma splices, and fragments:

- **Run-on sentences or comma splices.** Read until you find a complete thought. Then read the rest of the sentence. If the rest of the sentence is also a complete thought, separate the thoughts with a FANBOYS, a semicolon, or a period.

> Jenny, my fitness instructor at the gym, received an award for teaching (complete thought) she was so thrilled (another complete thought, so you need a FANBOYS, semicolon, or period to separate the thoughts).

- **Fragments.** Check to be sure you have a subject, a verb, *and* a complete thought.

> Edward, one of the nicest men I know (incomplete thought—so what about Edward?)
>
> asked me for a date. (Aah!)

Extra Help

A dependent clause has a subject and verb just like an independent clause, but it can't stand alone because it begins with a dependent word, such as *although*, *before*, or *when*. You'll find a complete list of dependent words in Appendix C: Useful Word Lists.

Parallel Phrasing

The rule of parallel phrasing states that we should use similar word patterns for similar ideas, either within a sentence or within a list of items. Unparallel phrasing is not only grammatically incorrect, it creates awkward sentences that distract readers from getting information clearly and accurately.

Parallel phrasing is a strategy that will:

- Untangle thoughts.
- Clarify relationships.
- Move sentences out of chaos and into order.

> **Unparallel:** I like biking, hiking, and to sail.
>
> **Parallel:** I like biking, hiking, and sailing.

> **Unparallel:** The audit focused on three criteria:
>
> 1. Employee-performance monitoring systems
> 2. How projects are managed
> 3. Organizational structure was also evaluated

> **Parallel:** The audit focused on three criteria:
>
> 1. Employee-performance monitoring systems
> 2. Project management
> 3. Organizational structure

Practice Sentences

For practice, take a look at the following sentences, and underline the subject once and the verb twice. You're looking for the subject and verb only in the *independent clause*. Although the dependent clauses may have subjects and verbs, they are not complete thoughts and so are not sentences. See the Answer Key at the end of this book for the results.

Example: If I had more time, I would travel more.

1. Before the football game at the stadium, we all ate dinner at Mary's.

2. The game can change in minutes because all the players are skilled.

3. Beside the pond, an egret waddled by on spindly legs.

4. Once she developed her thesis statement, the essay became easy to write.

5. He went to the soccer game even though he had lots of homework to do.

Practice Sentence Fixes

Test your ability to identify these possible missteps. In the following exercise, correct run-on sentences with a semicolon or a FANBOYS, and correct fragments by adding an independent clause. Remember—each sentence must have an independent clause. See the Answer Key at the end of this book for possible fixes.

Example: Although they had been friends for years.

                 Although they had been friends for years, they had an awful fight.

1. They were out playing he was studying.

2. After about 10 days in Italy.

3. I wanted to buy a little gondola, my mother wouldn't let me.

4. After our trip, which took almost two weeks.

5. If I had only studied for that English test.

Next Steps

As you become more proficient at writing sentences, you'll be amazed at what great essays you will build. In the next two chapters you'll learn how to make your sentences even better as we focus on the basic mechanics of language and on style.

7

Your Writer's Toolbox: Mechanics

Step 5: Prepare for Your Final Draft, Part 2

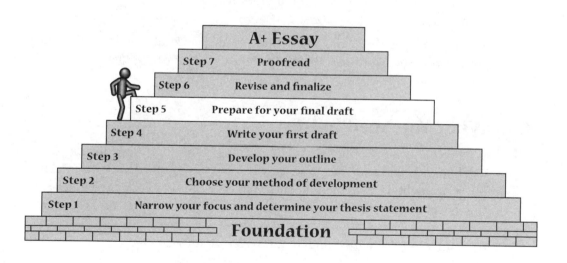

A+ Essay

Step 7	Proofread
Step 6	Revise and finalize
Step 5	Prepare for your final draft
Step 4	Write your first draft
Step 3	Develop your outline
Step 2	Choose your method of development
Step 1	Narrow your focus and determine your thesis statement

Foundation

You've made good progress in developing your essay. You're headed up the ladder, and your goal is in sight. On some steps, though, you might accidentally stumble over some debris. When the path is cluttered with problems in punctuation and grammar, the message becomes diluted. This chapter takes a brief look at spelling, punctuation, and grammar and at how some simple rules can ensure your sentences are written correctly.

Covered in This Chapter

- ☐ **Spelling.** Includes a few tips to ensure accurate spelling.
- ☐ **Key punctuation.** Shows the correct use of apostrophes, commas, and semicolons.
- ☐ **More on punctuation.** Provides further instruction on the correct use of colons, em dashes, hyphens, and quotation marks.
- ☐ **Grammar.** Includes a reminder on the importance of usage conventions such as proper verb agreement.

What You Need to Know

With errors in your spelling, punctuation, and grammar, you run the risk of losing two important things:

- *Your readers' attention.* Even minor mistakes distract readers from your message.

- *Your credibility.* If the small things aren't accurate, your readers may question the big things, like the points you are trying to make.

What You Need to Do

When you come to the phase of refining your text, knowing language mechanics helps ensure accuracy in what you've written. This is all information you might have learned recently, but take the time to review it, and use this chapter for reference when you have questions about the accuracy of your writing. For additional help, we suggest a number of useful resources in Appendix D: Writing, Grammar, and Word References.

Spelling

Accurate spelling is extremely important. This book will not discuss all the spelling rules, but you might find the list of Words Most Often Misspelled in Appendix C, Useful Word Lists, helpful.

To correct misspellings, you need to read your work carefully and find errors. The problem is that, often, you don't recognize the error. Having someone else read your essay can help.

Alert

If you are unsure of the spelling of a word or name, never assume it's correct because you think you know how it's spelled or you found it in a print or online resource. Take the time to look it up.

You might think, "I can use spell-check and that will take care of letting me know what is misspelled. Not so! Spell-check would see nothing wrong with the following sentence.

When we saw there knew hose, we liked the floor pan but we're knot impressed with the decorations.

Extra Help

As a spelling aid, buy a small address book. When you misspell a word or are unsure of the spelling of a word, enter that word in the alphabetical portion of the address book. You can then look it up later and be aware of words you, personally, tend to misspell—and you have your own private spelling book!

Key Punctuation

The major problems with punctuation come from misuse of apostrophes, commas, and semicolons. Knowledge of how to effectively use these punctuation marks will make your writing clearer and stronger. After we look closely at these three, we will review some of the other marks that might give you trouble.

Apostrophes

Apostrophes serve two functions:

- To show ownership
- To form contractions

Ownership. To indicate that something belongs to John, we use an apostrophe:

> John's dog
>
> The boy's coat

What if there is more than one owner? Then we show it this way:

> The children's dog
>
> The boys' coats (several boys have coats)

Contractions. When you leave out a letter or letters, use an apostrophe to show where the letters are missing.

> I'd (I would) have gone, but I didn't (did not) have time.
>
> The first ebook reader was released in the '90s.

Exception: Only one word changes spelling completely with an apostrophe. There's no logical reason why *will not* does not become *willn't*, but it doesn't. It changes to *won't*.

Four sets of words give most people trouble when it comes to apostrophes. To help you remember these easily, we've developed a little chart we call the WITY words.

WITY Words

CONTRACTION	POSSESSION
Who's (Who is)	Whose
It's (It is)	Its
They're (They are)	Their
You're (You are)	Your

These sentences might make it easier to remember the WITY Words.

> **Wh**o's coming to dinner and whose book is that?
>
> **It**'s late, but the parrot needs its supper.
>
> **Th**ey're late, but that is generally their habit.
>
> **Yo**u're right, but your manner is offensive.

Commas

The comma serves as a great clarifier. It separates elements in a sentence to help the reader make sense of what is written. It is used in several ways:

- To separate items in a series
- To indicate a natural pause
- To set off extra information
- To separate introductory material

Items in a Series. If you jumble everything together, the reader will get lost. The series comma helps.

> For breakfast I usually have yogurt with bananas, papaya, kiwi, and bran cereal.

The commas show that the writer adds four things to the yogurt. Otherwise, you might indicate you had a banana-papaya in your yogurt. There is some controversy about whether you need the comma before "and," but go with the style your teacher wants or that you choose—just remember to be consistent in whichever style you choose.

A Natural Pause. At times you want your reader to stop and consider what you said. Since a comma indicates a pause, you can use it to intensify your message.

> Yes, indeed, I will stop for pizza on the way home.

The commas here show how delighted you will be to pick up the pizza.

To Set Off Extra Information. When you add explanatory information, if it all runs together, the reader will get lost. These sections, set off by commas, can be lifted out of the sentence and the sentence will still make sense:

Harry, after doing his homework, went to the movies with his friends.

To Separate Introductory Material. Sentences introduced by words such as *after*, *although*, *because*, *since*, *when*, *then*, and *while* need a comma after the introductory word or phrase:

When I got my Kindle, I started reading more.

Although she studied hard, she only made a B on the test.

Remember

Commas add sense to your writing. Use them when NOT using them makes your writing hard to understand.

Semicolons

Although not used often, semicolons serve an important purpose. When you have two complete thoughts, you can use a semicolon rather than a FAN-BOYS to provide the proper separation.

I went to the club early last night; Kathy wasn't there yet.

Alert

A comma can never separate two complete thoughts; use a semicolon instead.

You also use a semicolon in a series where commas are a part of the list:

She has lived in Moscow, Russia; Venice, Italy; Madrid, Spain; and now lives in Lima, Peru.

More on Punctuation

Following are brief guidelines on a few more punctuation marks you will find useful.

Colon

Colons are used to introduce a thought or list that follows:

> Three things will make you successful: reading, listening, and asking for help.

Em dash

The em dash is used to signal a dramatic break in thoughts and often as a replacement for the colon. On computers, with the default settings, an em dash is created automatically when you type two hyphens.

> I arrived in Hawaii—the land of gentle breezes and sunshine—and it was raining.

> I packed and made sure I had everything—shoes, purses, dresses, and swimwear.

Hyphen

The hyphen has many uses:

- Before a noun, with two or more words that describe it (*a well-traveled highway, a strong-willed woman*)

- Where misreading is possible (*re-creation* versus *recreation, small-business owner* versus *small business owner*)

- With "self" and "ex" (*self-confident, ex-senator*)

- In two-word spelled-out numbers (*thirty-one, fifty-five*)

- In most terms that have three or more parts (*sister-in-law*)

Quotation Marks

Quotation marks are also needed in different circumstances:

- When quoting from another source

  Gertrude Stein is famous for saying, "A rose is a rose is a rose."

- To show someone is speaking

  The teacher said, again, "The test will be tomorrow."

- When you're using a word or phrase in a special, often sarcastic, context

  When asked how he liked the movie he said it was "nice."

- To signify titles of short works, songs, poems, or plays

  In the book *O'Henry Stories,* "The Gift of the Magi" is one of my favorites.

Place quotation marks in the following manner:

- Outside commas and periods

  He said, "I'd love to live in Boston."

- Inside colons and semicolons

  She commented, "He's late again"; I just can't stand it.

- Inside dashes, question marks, and exclamation points when referring to quoted material and outside when they refer to the rest of the sentence

  Kevin asked, "Are you sure you want to go there?"

  How could she answer anything but, "I certainly do"?

Alert

These rules for where to place quotation marks are correct for American usage. British usage rules place the quotation marks *inside* commas and periods. (He said, "I'd love to live in Boston".)

Extra Help

Single quotation marks are used in only one situation—when quoting within a quote. (He announced, "I go by the name 'the Avenger' to my friends.") British practice, on the other hand, allows the reverse use of double and single quotation marks in such instances.

Grammar

Clear communication matters. People have agreed to stick to certain conventions so that they all speak the same language and understand each other. You need to use the language in a way that your readers will understand. There are a number of excellent grammar books to guide you through proper usage. We've listed several excellent references in Appendix D: Writing, Grammar, and Word References.

Though we are not covering grammar in-depth here, there is one area that seems to be the most problematic for people—*agreement*, especially with subjects and verbs, pronouns, and tense. Following are some helpful hints on how to handle agreement correctly.

Agreement

All parts of a sentence should agree. In general, if the subject is singular, the verb should be singular. If the subject is plural, the verb should be plural.

> *Each* of the boys *has* his own locker.
>
> *Both* of the boys *have* their own lockers.

The following words are singular and take a singular verb:

one	nobody	each
anyone	anybody	either
someone	somebody	neither
everyone	everybody	

One of my friends *is* a rapper.

Each of the students *is* responsible for one report.

Either of the girls *is* a good choice.

The following "group" words take a singular verb if you are referring to the group as a whole, but they take a plural verb if you are referring to the individuals in the group:

group	committee	team
family	class	dozen
kind	number	public
audience		

My family *is* on my side.   My family *are* all scientists.

A dozen *is* enough   A dozen *are* going.

Not only should subject and verb agree. A pronoun, too, should agree with the word it refers to. If that word is singular, the pronoun should be singular. If that word is plural, the pronoun should be plural.

Each of the boys has *his* own locker.

Both of the boys have *their* own lockers.

If you have trouble deciding whether a verb should be singular or plural, put *he* or *they* in front of it. For example, if you are wondering whether to write *my teachers agree* or *my teachers agrees*, try putting *he* or *they* in front of the verb.

he agrees

they agree

Thus you will know that *my teachers agree* is correct.

Modern usage allows some exceptions to the rules for agreement, especially in conversation. Sometimes, for example, the verb and the pronoun may agree with the intent of the subject rather than with its grammatical form.

Everybody took off their hats as the parade went by. (The intent of the sentence is to show that all the people took off their hats, and therefore a plural pronoun is used.)

Today many people write *he or she* and *him or her* in an attempt to avoid sex bias, but such writing can be awkward and wordy. To avoid such wordiness, the pronouns *they, them,* and *their* are frequently used, particularly in conversation.

A better way to avoid the awkward *he or she* and *him or her* is to make the words plural. Instead of writing "Each of the students was in *his or her* place," write "All of the *students* were in *their* places," thus avoiding sex bias and still having a grammatically correct sentence. We discuss this more thoroughly in the "Gender-Free Writing" section of Chapter 8.

Although nonstandard forms are acceptable in conversation, they are not acceptable in formal writing. For your school writing, therefore, stick with the strict grammatical rules.

Extra Help on Pronouns

Like verbs, pronouns change depending on how they're used. They must agree in number and gender with the noun they replace.

The *boys* took the *books* home.

They took *them* home.

Determining which pronoun to use depends on one of these functions:

SUBJECT	OBJECT	POSSESSIVE
I	me	my/mine
you	you	your/yours
he/she/it	him/her/it	his/her(s)/its
they	them	their(s)

The subject pronoun is the noun *doing* the action. The object pronoun is the noun *receiving* the action. The possessive *shows ownership* of the noun.

I (subject) gave *him* (object) *his* (possessive) letter.

One of the biggest challenges with possessives comes when there are two subjects or objects.

> John and Rose went shopping.
>
> John and *she* went shopping.

The secret to solving this replacement is to leave off the first person and see if it makes sense. "John and her went shopping" may sound right, but you wouldn't say, "her went shopping." Remembering what noun you're replacing determines what pronoun you use.

Practice Agreement

Accurate agreement is important not only to follow the rules but also to help the reader clearly understand your intended message. In each of the first set of sentences here, choose which underlined word accurately fits the sentence. Notice how lack of agreement can make the sentence confusing—and sometimes actually incorrect. See the Answer Key at the end of this book for the correct answers.

1. Caleb is one of those people who <u>enjoy/enjoys</u> reading.
2. <u>Completing/Having completed</u> the tournament, Barbara took the next flight.
3. As the cells divide, a series of events <u>is/are</u> set into motion.
4. Coffee and milk <u>is/are</u> best with breakfast.
5. Neither the prices nor the quality <u>has/have</u> changed.

Now correct the following sentences so all elements are in agreement.

1. Continuous improvement means studying, practicing, and a commitment of time to your goal.
2. If you had asked me how I painted, I would say with bright and bold colors.
3. She sang louder than him.

Extra Help with Verbs

Verbs can be troublesome because they have many forms and must agree with both the subject and the tense (past, present, future, and then there's the past participle). The one rule that gives people a lot of trouble is that *third person singular, present tense, takes an "s" on the verb*. But what does that mean? Let's break this down:

First person is *I*.

Second person is *you*.

Third person is *all other nouns*.

Singular means one.

Present tense means happening now.

Look at these examples:

I take Spanish.

You take Spanish.

Mary *takes* Spanish classes on Monday.

We usually think of using *s* to indicate plural, but in this case *s* means singular.

Practice Punctuation

Add the missing punctuation to the following seven sentences. See the Answer Key at the end of this book for the correct answers.

1. A wonderful thing happened last night my friends gave me a surprise birthday party.

2. If you are in a hurry use a quick drying glue for the top layer

3. The director Sophia lives in San Francisco but all the actors live in New York.

4. The new manager was confident that a crisis could be averted the workers having witnessed this sort of predicament before were not so sure.

5. I enjoyed the movie *Chariots of Fire* but some people thought it was dull

6. Not many people know that the song Happy Birthday was written in 1893.

7. Every question you ask should be three things clear concise and polite.

Next Steps

This chapter has discussed the importance of accurate spelling, punctuation, and grammar. Proper use will make your writing clearer and more coherent and leave your readers informed and satisfied. Now we'll move to the third valuable tool in your writer's toolbox—style.

8

Your Writer's Toolbox: Style

Step 5: Prepare for Your Final Draft, Part 3

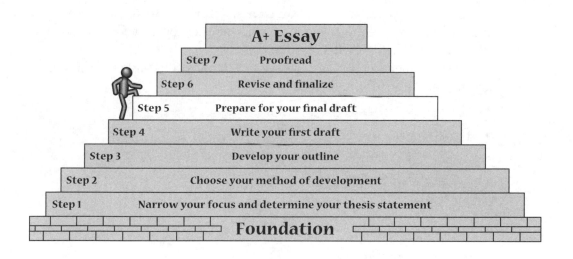

A+ Essay

Step 7	Proofread
Step 6	Revise and finalize
Step 5	Prepare for your final draft
Step 4	Write your first draft
Step 3	Develop your outline
Step 2	Choose your method of development
Step 1	Narrow your focus and determine your thesis statement

Foundation

Style is the third batch of tools in Your Writer's Toolbox. Taking the time to give your words, your sentences, and, ultimately, your essay additional attention elevates the level of your writing. In this chapter you'll learn some of the "tools of the trade" to give your writing flair, as well as language to avoid and tips for writing that grabs your readers' attention.

Covered in This Chapter

- [ ] **Guidelines for stronger writing.** Use precise vocabulary, active verbs, vivid examples, and active voice; avoid "to be" verbs and expletive sentences; be aware of connotation, coherence, and conciseness.
- [ ] **Giving your writing extra flair.** Use similies, metaphors, and analogies.
- [ ] **Language to avoid.** Watch out for wordiness, redundancy, clichés, and mixed metaphors.
- [ ] **Gender-free writing.** Avoid sexism.
- [ ] **Twelve tips for compelling writing.** Keep in mind some keys to interesting writing.

What You Need to Know

Style is the combination of the words you use and the way you put them together. Just as we dress in our own style, we write in our own style. Remember, however, that you are always writing for an audience, so your style must be one that will appeal to them.

These elements contribute to a style that grabs your audience's attention and makes them want to read on.

- Use precise vocabulary.
- Use strong, active verbs.
- Avoid "to be" verbs.
- Avoid expletive sentences.
- Use vivid examples.
- Be aware of connotation.
- Check for coherence.
- Be concise.
- Use active voice.

What You Need to Do

Writing is more interesting and fun to read when it shows the writer's personality and emotion. Use these guidelines to make your writing stronger and more interesting.

Guidelines for Stronger Writing

Strong writing, also referred to as a *strong voice*, not only enhances your effectiveness in conveying your message to your audience but also helps make you and your message more memorable. To maintain a strong voice in your writing, show your unique personality by choosing language that brings your ideas to life.

Use Precise Vocabulary

Vocabulary means the choice of words. Too often, people use the first word that comes to mind, and that word is either overused or not precise.

> **Vague:** Our yoga instructor Lexa exhibits boundless energy.

This is sufficient, but it does not convey what you mean by *energy*.

> **Better:** Lexa's animation keeps us all upbeat.

This is more precise.

An excellent text to improve your vocabulary is *A Cure for the Common Word* by K.D. Sullivan (McGraw-Hill, 2007). An excerpt from this book is included in Appendix C: Useful Word Lists to help you go beyond using common, overused words and instead incorporate more creative and precise words into your writing.

Use Strong, Active Verbs

The strength of any sentence should be in the verbs you use. Verbs show action, and the more precise the verb, the better the readers see what's happening.

> **Vague:** The teacher walked into the classroom.

This conveys the information, but there's no picture.

Better: The teacher *strolled/hurried/ambled* into the classroom.

If you replace *walked* with a more descriptive verb—*strolled*, *hurried*, or *ambled*, for example—the readers have a better picture.

Avoid "To Be" Verbs

A verb, by itself, is a part of speech. When referring to a verb, however, we use the infinitive (preceded with "to"). The verb "to be" is called irregular because it doesn't follow the general rules for verbs and has these forms:

PRESENT TENSE	PAST TENSE
I am	I was
You are	You were
He/she/it is	He/she/it was
We are	We were
They are	They were

Why do you need to know this? Most people use too many "to be" verbs in their writing. This presents a problem because the verbs show no action and, therefore, make the writing flat. For example:

I know a man who is very mysterious. (Isn't very interesting.)

I know a mysterious man. (Much better, to the point.)

I know a man who seems mysterious. ("To be" verb is replaced, giving a slightly different—and more intriguing—meaning to the sentence.)

If you do no more to improve your writing than take out as many "to be" verbs as you can, you will immediately liven it up.

Avoid Expletive Sentences

An expletive sentence starts with one of the following:

- There are
- There is
- There was
- There were

- It is
- It was

When you begin a sentence with one of these, the sentence has two strikes against it. In each of these cases, the writer has used a form of the "to be" verb (*are, is, was, were*), which you now know should be avoided. Even more damaging, these phrases delay letting us know who or what the subject is, so you have to wait to even know who or what the writer is talking about.

> There is a nice guy in my class. (boring)
>
> I met a nice guy in my class. (better)

Again, if you alter these sentences, along with eliminating the "to be" verbs, you will have made giant steps in improving your writing.

Use Vivid Examples

The more you can engage your readers, the more likely it is that they will read on. If you can be exact, and get the readers involved, you will communicate better:

> The little dog ate the doggie treat.

This may be clear, but it does not draw a striking picture.

> The little brown-and-white cocker spaniel munched on the Milk Bone I gave her.

Much better. Now the readers can see more exactly what you see.

Be Aware of Connotation

Denotation is a word's definition. When you go to the dictionary, you find the denotation of the word. Many words also have a connotation. *Connotation* means the emotional appeal the word has. If you tell your friend that she is skinny she may not take that as a compliment. But, if you tell her she's slender you'll get a much more positive reaction.

Not every word has a connotation, but using words with positive connotations can turn a negative reaction into a positive one. For example, if you call a man domineering, he may be offended, but if you call him strong or positive, he will be pleased. Many females object strongly to being called "girl." To them it connotes someone not grown and not very forceful. So consider your audience and choose those words that will keep them interested and on your side.

Check for Coherence

If your readers cannot follow what you're talking about, they probably won't read on. So often, you know what you mean and have pieced it all together in your own mind, but you don't manage to get the connections down in your writing. You may do something like this:

> We went to Disneyland last weekend. Mother had to find her swimsuit. Dad got the car checked out. We left at 8:00 A.M. The trip took eight hours. We had a hard time finding a motel. We hadn't made reservations.

This gives the information but in jumbled manner. It's much better to say:

> We decided to go to Disneyland this weekend. Dad got the car checked out to make sure we had no trouble on the way. We decided to leave at 8:00 A.M. since that would get us there in time to settle in. We didn't make it at 8:00 because Mother couldn't find her bathing suit, but we were delayed only an hour. On the road at last, we had a smooth trip. It got rocky, however, when my parents discovered neither had made a reservation. We were lucky. We found a motel, had dinner, and got ready for our big day.

Now the information has been expanded to a full developmental paragraph. The order is clear, and we can sense both the excitement and problems of the trip.

Extra Help

It's not enough that in your mind, *you* know the connections. You need to help the readers follow along. Words like *then*, *later*, *after*, and *next* can help keep readers on track.

Be Concise

One danger that might arise as you're trying to use vivid examples and add coherence to your writing is that you start writing too much. Most readers don't have a lot of time and want you to make your point quickly and effectively.

Following is an excellent definition for concise writing from William Strunk Jr. in *Elements of Style*:

> Vigorous writing is concise. A sentence should contain no unnecessary words, a paragraph no unnecessary sentences, for the same reason that a drawing should have no unnecessary lines and a machine no unnecessary parts. This requires not that the writer make all his sentences short, or that he avoid all detail and treat his subjects only in outline, but that every word tell.

In the following example, note that the wording in italics gives extra information, but instead of it giving additional value to the description, it actually distracts the reader from what the writer most wants to convey.

> My sister and I awoke to Mom standing in the doorway to our room. *It was 7 o'clock in the morning.* She told us to gather together a few of the things most important to us. *We started to think if we should pick our tea set, or our rock collection, or something else.* We were moving to a small room at our grandmother's house that day and probably would never come back to this house.

Use Active Voice

Verbs show whether a subject performs the action, called *active voice*, or whether the subject is receiving the action, called *passive voice*. The active voice forms a more powerful sentence, especially since the passive voice uses a "to be" verb. Whenever possible, use the active voice.

> Using computers is easy for most teenagers.

You don't know who or what is the subject until the last word in the sentence, so it's not very interesting.

Most teenagers find using computers very easy.

Much better. Now, immediately, we know who is doing what.

Giving Your Writing Extra Flair

The best writers use language that goes beyond what is accurate, or even helpful. As we've noted earlier, words and images should draw in your readers, get them involved, make them part of what you're saying, and make them want to read more. Following are a few of the tools professional writers use—and you can, too.

One good way to communicate is by using figurative language or figures of speech. Such language paints pictures in readers' minds, allowing them to see and understand a point more readily and clearly. Here are three devices you can use.

Similies use *like, as if,* or *as though* to make a clear comparison between two seemingly different things.

The frozen ocean stretched to the horizon *like* a white desert.

A *metaphor* expresses the unfamiliar in terms of the familiar.

His *hawkish* features intrigued me.

Analogies compare similar features of two dissimilar things; they explain something unfamiliar by relating it to something familiar.

Writing an essay can be compared to preparing to participate in a sport. You have to have the proper equipment, practice, and be prepared for problems. If you're in great shape and well prepared, you will win.

Language to Avoid: Wordiness and Redundancy

Many writers are unaware of how "cluttered" writing can become. Wordiness and redundancy are two of the most common problems in writing, and they will lull your readers to sleep if left unchecked.

To avoid this issue, carefully review your essay for redundancies and wordiness. Check to see if there are ways to say things—just as effectively—in one or two words instead of six or seven. If there are words that do not add anything, remove them. The goal is to make every word count, so keep the words that enhance your message, and delete the ones that might distract your readers.

Following are a few examples of wordiness and redundancy, as well as suggested alternatives for each phrase.

Wordiness List

at this point in time	now
in the field of	in
for the purpose of	to
due to the fact that	because
in the not too distant future	soon
in view of the fact that	since
in spite of the fact that	although
fully cognizant of	aware
enclosed herewith please find	enclosed

Redundancy List

small in size	small
join together	join
advanced planning	planning
assembled together	assembled
cooperate together	cooperate
rarely ever	rarely
the present incumbent	the incumbent
my personal choice	my choice
return back	return

Clichés and Mixed Metaphors

A *cliché* is an overused figure of speech, such as *busy as a bee*. We use clichés all the time, and many are useful as shorthand for familiar ideas. But if you use them to excess in your writing, readers are likely to conclude that what you are saying is not very new or interesting—or true.

Mixed metaphors use images that are inconsistent:

> All at once he was alone in this noisy hive with no place to roost. (Tom Wolfe, *The Bonfire of the Vanities*)

Since bees don't roost, *hive* and *roost* are inconsistent in this sentence.

Gender-Free Writing

Compound nouns containing *man* and *men* as an element have traditionally been used generically to refer to males and females alike:

> Not for the average layman
>
> Concerning all businessmen
>
> Increase the number of man-hours
>
> A new source of manpower

The generic use of such terms may be offensive to many people who feel that the masculine bias of these terms makes them unsuitable for reference to women as well as men. Therefore, avoid such terms whenever possible. Here are some suggested substitutes:

Instead of	Try
mankind	people
man	person
manmade	manufactured, constructed, synthetic
manpower	workers, labor, human energy
salesman	salesperson, sales clerk, sales representative
fireman	firefighter
waiter	waitperson
foreman	supervisor

Also avoid singular masculine pronouns:

> **Sexist:** If *an employee* will be working with hazardous materials, *he* must complete the required safety courses.
>
> **Better:** If *an employee* will be working with hazardous materials, *he or she* must complete the required safety courses.
>
> **Preferred:** If *employees* will be working with hazardous materials, *they* must complete the required safety courses.

Twelve Tips for Compelling Writing

When writing, you have a lot to remember and consider. If you get to a point where you're feeling overwhelmed, these 12 key tips will give you some guidance.

1. **Be brief.** Keep content—and titles—as short as possible to catch and hold readers' attention.

2. **Be specific.** For powerful, precise communication, get right to the point and say just what you mean. Instead of "We had lots of homework this week," say, "We had to read 60 pages of homework."

3. **Limit pronouns as sentence subjects.** Where possible, use nouns as the subjects of sentences. *It* and *they* can be ambiguous. "The dog chased the cat. It ran very fast." Which is the speedy one?

4. **Use a variety of sentences.** To make your essays more interesting, use a mixture of sentence types to vary your sentence structure and length.

5. **Put important content first.** The topic sentence sets up the content, and then the rest of the paragraph explains it.

6. **Stick to a single topic.** Try to discuss just one thing per paragraph.

7. **Know and target your audience.** Tailor your message to the knowledge and needs of your readers. Remember to define terms for those not familiar with them.

8. **Address readers with "you."** Involve your readers by speaking to them directly. "When you plant a tree, you must water it."

9. **Make it active, not passive.** Focus on who's doing it, not on what's done. Say "He called her," not "She was called by him." Unless the "doer" really doesn't matter, you'll save words and keep your readers awake.

10. **Be respectful.** Take care to avoid unintended insults and slights. Be alert to racial, ethnic, or gender bias in your words. "He or she" and "him or her" are here to stay. "They" and "their" (with a singular antecedent) are taking up residence, too.

11. **Use positives, not negatives.** Tell readers what they should do, not what they shouldn't do. Say "Please be prompt" instead of "Don't be late." It's powerful psychology—one stresses the desired outcome, the other its opposite.

12. **Leave your readers satisfied.** Ensure you have achieved your writing goal—to inform, to explain, or to persuade.

Practice Avoiding "To Be" Verbs

Change the following sentences by replacing the "to be" verbs with active verbs. See the Answer Key at the end of this book for possible answers.

> Example: There is an ostrich eating oranges in my backyard.
>
> Becomes: I saw an ostrich eating oranges in my backyard.

1. The decision to expand was made by the chairman.
2. It was late when I arrived at the bazaar.
3. My last exam, fortunately, was the easiest.
4. When my sister bought tickets to the concert, I was astonished.
5. If I had known I was going to get the job, I would have bought an iPhone.

Practice Passive to Active Voice and Avoiding Wordiness

Following are passive sentences that would work better as active sentences. Rewrite to change them from passive to active. Concentrate on explaining who or what performs the action. A tip: Most often active writing uses fewer words than passive writing, thus minimizing unnecessary wordiness. See the Answer Key at the end of this book for possible answers.

1. With the use of the right tools, the chair can be fixed quickly. (13 words)
2. When a fan is moved back and forth, a pressure is produced by the motion at every point the fan passes, which is observed as a soft breeze being created. (30 words)
3. Judgment should be exercised in laying out the steps of the process so that the plan is shown as practical. (20 words)

Next Steps

Now that you've reviewed the tools in Your Writer's Toolbox, you're ready to sit down with your first draft and create your final draft. As a further aid at this point, look over Appendix B: Grammar and Usage Glossary of Terms. Now there are only two steps left. The next chapter will guide you through the revision process, as you incorporate all you've learned so far.

9

Your Final Draft Checklist

Step 6: Revise and Finalize

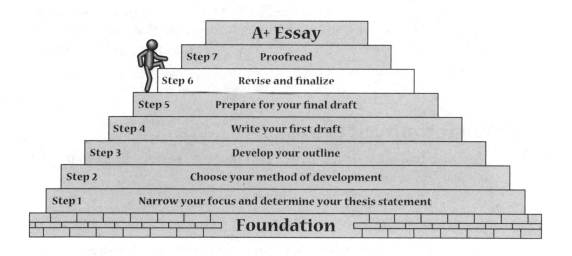

Now that you are equipped with all the tools you need to create a well-written, effective, engaging essay and have worked your way up the ladder one step at a time . . . you're almost at the top. It's time to revise your first draft—putting all you've learned into use—and write your final draft.

Covered in This Chapter

☐ **The revision process.** Think about how to improve your writing.
☐ **The review process.** Look over your writing to make it even better.
☐ **Three-stage review checklist.** Watch for content, accuracy, and style.

The Revision Process

To revise, according to *Merriam-Webster's Collegiate Dictionary, 11th Edition,* means "to look over again in order to correct or improve." It also means "to see again." And that's what you'll be doing—seeing your writing again, not just a second time, but in a new way.

 ## What You Need to Know

Earlier chapters have given you the information you now need to turn your first rough draft into a polished final draft. It's time to put those lessons into practice. This chapter guides you through the steps of revising your first draft and provides a checklist of items to be aware of as you go through your revision process.

 ## What You Need to Do

In preparation for starting the revision process, consider these important tips that will help you in this next step:

Choose the Best Time and Place

Some people need complete quiet when they work, and some people can work with the TV or music on. Even if you fall into this latter category, when it's time for you to concentrate on finalizing your essay, find a place to work that is quiet, comfortable, and well lit.

Also, you know yourself and your work habits better than anyone else. And you know what time of day you're most productive. If possible, don't put yourself in a time crunch where you are forced to work at times when your energy is low. Work when you are most likely to be alert, focused, and creative.

Your Work Tools

You probably created your first draft using a word-processing program. If you work well and creatively revising completely on the computer, that's great and will save you time. But if you know that you organize and think better looking at your words in print, don't hesitate to take the time to print out your essay (double-spaced) and make your revisions in print before typing them into the electronic file.

Even if you work on paper first, you'll be surprised at what you decide to edit or revise when you're typing in your changes. That's okay. It's all a process.

In addition to your computer, have a good dictionary and style manuals handy—either print versions or trusted websites, like:

- *Merriam-Webster's Collegiate Dictionary* or Merriam-Webster Online (merriam-webster.com)

- *The Chicago Manual of Style* or chicagomanualofstyle.org

See Appendix D: Writing, Grammar, and Word References for a more complete list of book references.

Take Short Breaks

It's human nature to want to stick with something until it's finished. And there is great merit in staying focused on your goal. At the same time, if you're overtired, you don't concentrate as well, you aren't as sharp, and everything you do takes longer. Instead of working hours at a time, take a break at least every hour, even if it's only for a few minutes. This will refresh your body and your mind. And if you find, for whatever reason, you just can't stay focused on what you're doing, either take a break or work on a different part of the project that's easier and less taxing—like putting your bibliography together.

The Review Process

People work best in different ways. Following is a three-step process that has proved successful. If you feel a different process will work better for you, then follow your natural pattern. The key is that no matter *how* you work, you want to keep moving forward and not let yourself get stopped.

When you try to do too many things at one time, it's harder to do all of them well. For that reason, review and revise in stages:

1. In the first stage, read through your essay by paying attention to the *content* you've included as opposed to looking for typos and accuracy of sentence structure or improving the style of writing. If you notice errors and can quickly correct them, of course do so, but don't make accuracy your focus at this point. Instead, focus on content.

2. Next, read through your essay again. This time you do want to focus on *accuracy*. Focus on correcting spelling, grammar, and punctuation errors or improving the style of writing. You'll still need to do a final proofread, but by paying attention to several of these items now, your final proofread will take less time and you will be more accurate.

3. Now read your essay one more time with an eye to adding appropriate elements of *style* as we discussed in Chapter 8 to bring your writing to a higher level.

It may seem like it will take a long time to go through your work in stages, but you'll be surprised how quickly it goes when you're focusing on one area of review at a time.

Three-Stage Review Checklist

The following checklist will help prompt you for items to consider in each stage of your review.

Content

The Subject

☐ Did I stay focused on the subject of my essay?

☐ Was I clear on the purpose of my essay—to inform, explain, or persuade?

Title

☐ Does the title grab the readers' attention?

☐ Does the title give a clue as to what my essay is about?

Introductory Paragraph

☐ Does the introductory paragraph capture the readers' attention?

☐ Does the introductory paragraph have 3–5 sentences ending in a clear thesis statement?

☐ Does my thesis statement have both a subject and a controlling idea?

☐ Does the introductory paragraph include at least one of these:
  - Ask an intriguing question.
  - Use a startling fact.
  - Use a quote.
  - Tell a story.

☐ Did I maintain my chosen method of development throughout?

Developmental Paragraphs

☐ Does each developmental paragraph have a clearly stated topic sentence?

☐ Is each topic sentence directly related to my thesis statement?

☐ Does each developmental paragraph contain 3 points with 2–3 sentences per point, and a concluding sentence?

☐ Is each developmental paragraph fully developed with the major and minor points needed?

☐ Do I have sufficient and accurate details and facts—like names, dates, statistics—that make the main ideas in each paragraph clear?

☐ Do any of my ideas need more support?

☐ Did I provide clear connections between sentences?

☐ Did I provide clear connections between paragraphs?

Concluding Paragraph

☐ Do I have 2–3 sentences that accomplish one of these:
  - Wrap up my ideas.
  - Restate my thesis statement in a new way.
  - Give a brief summary of the subject.
  - Leave my readers something to think about.
  - Call my readers to an action.

Accuracy

Spelling and Capitalization

☐ Are proper names, common words, and special terms spelled and capitalized correctly?

☐ Are shortened forms (abbreviations and acronyms) spelled and capitalized correctly and defined when first used or as needed?

Grammar

- ☐ Do subjects and verbs agree (I work, he works)?
- ☐ Are verbs in correct tense (I work, I worked, I had worked)?
- ☐ Do pronouns agree in gender and number with what (or whom) they refer to (Tom and Bill rode *their* bikes; the tree dropped *its* leaves)?
- ☐ Are there run-on sentences, comma splices, or fragments?

Punctuation

- ☐ Is there missing, duplicated, or misplaced punctuation?
- ☐ Are apostrophes used only for possessives (Jane's) and missing letters (I'll; rock 'n' roll), not for plurals (two Janes; 1900s)?
- ☐ Do apostrophes face the correct way ('04, *not* '04)?
- ☐ Is a comma used before the last item in a series (Tom, Dick, and Harry) or not, whichever style I've chosen, but used the same throughout?
- ☐ Is a comma, without a connecting conjunction, not used to separate two complete sentences (use stronger punctuation, like a period or semicolon, instead)?
- ☐ Are em dashes (—) used correctly—in pairs if they're in the middle of a sentence?
- ☐ Are there always opening *and* closing parentheses and brackets?
- ☐ Is the period *inside* parentheses when the parentheses enclose a separate and complete sentence?
- ☐ Is the period *outside* parentheses when the parenthetical matter— even a complete sentence—is included in *another* sentence?
- ☐ Are there always opening *and* closing quotation marks as appropriate?
- ☐ Are single quotation marks used only around a quote within a quote? (British usage differs.)
- ☐ Are periods and commas inside quotation marks? (British usage differs.)
- ☐ Are semicolons and colons outside quotation marks?
- ☐ Is other punctuation inside or outside quotation marks, depending on whether it's part of the quoted item?
- ☐ Are words separated by one (and only one) space?
- ☐ Are periods and colons followed by only one space?
- ☐ In electronic copy, do web links in text work correctly?
- ☐ Is the bibliography complete?

Style

☐ Do my sentences vary in type and length?

☐ Do I include too many details?

☐ Is each paragraph complete, or do I stop before I make my point?

☐ What can I cut from my essay?

☐ Do I repeat myself? Perhaps I made the same point twice or use the same phrase too often.

☐ Do I just say too much?

☐ Do all my sentences make sense?

☐ Do all the words work together to make a point?

☐ Do I repeat the same verbs or adjectives?

☐ Do I need to reorganize in my essay?

☐ Do all my sentences sound alike?

☐ Does my essay have a clear beginning, middle, and end?

☐ Do I maintain parallel phrasing—using similar word patterns for similar ideas?

☐ Do I use precise vocabulary?

☐ Do I use strong, active verbs?

☐ Did I minimize use of "to be" verbs?

☐ Did I eliminate expletive sentences?

☐ Do I use vivid examples?

☐ Was I aware of connotations, using them appropriately?

☐ Is my text coherent?

☐ Was I concise in my writing?

☐ Do I use similes, metaphors, and analogies for extra flair?

☐ Have I avoided wordiness, redundancy, clichés, and mixed metaphors?

☐ Do I use gender-free writing?

☐ Did I follow the Twelve Tips for Compelling Writing?

1. Be brief.
2. Be specific.
3. Limit pronouns as sentence subjects.
4. Use a variety of sentences.
5. Put important content first.
6. Stick to a single topic.
7. Know and target your audience.
8. Address readers with "you."

9. Make it active, not passive.
10. Be respectful.
11. Use positives, not negatives.
12. Leave your readers satisfied.

Next Steps

As you revise and rewrite, remember that finding things in your essay that need to be fixed is not a sign that you're a bad writer. It means that some sections of your writing need more attention. And, it means that you are careful enough to notice such problems. Congratulate yourself for that. Now go on to hone your skills as you proofread your essay.

10

A Final Look

Step 7: Proofread

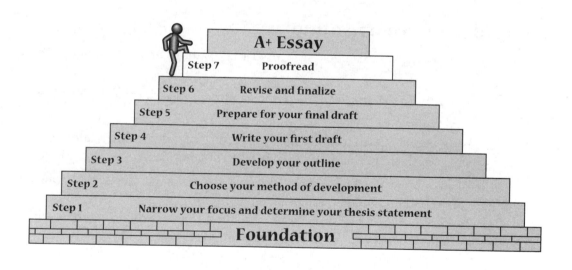

Proofreading is essential in everything you write. In today's world, people tend not to proofread e-mails, text messages, tweets, and so on, and with your friends, that's acceptable. But anytime you are writing where it matters how you are perceived, presenting your ideas in a clear, correct, and consistent manner gives the impression you know what you're talking about and care about what you say. Others will then care, also. Proofreading gives your writing that final polish to make your work shine.

Covered in This Chapter

- ☐ **The value of proofreading.** Allows for accurate work so your reader is not distracted by errors and is confident in the value of your ideas.
- ☐ **What is proofreading?** Read carefully to look for errors in spelling, grammar, punctuation, and sense and readability.
- ☐ **Checking the Three Cs.** Ensures your work is clear, correct, and consistent.
- ☐ **Proofread in stages.** Following a methodical process helps you more easily catch errors.

When you're pressed for time, proofreading may seem unnecessary, but omitting it can have serious consequences. This chapter will help you understand why, and show you how to proofread like a professional.

The Value of Proofreading

As noted earlier in this book, if your writing contains errors, you have a lot to lose:

- **The readers' attention.** Even minor mistakes distract the readers from your message.
- **Your credibility.** If the small things aren't accurate, your readers may question the big things—like the validity of your idea.

Okay, you say. But I have a spell-checker, a grammar-checker, and even a thesaurus on my computer. Isn't that enough?

Well, no. There's far more to proofreading than looking for typos, and even some of those will slip by your software, like these classics:

The speaker apologized for being a little horse.

The contract becomes effective after we all sing it.

It takes a human being to catch blunders such as those and to keep things consistent—no software program will prevent you from using *Professor* Dyson in one place and *professor* Dyson someplace else.

Proofreading is crucial to your writing, and it certainly takes attention to do it, but it doesn't have to be daunting. It's a simple routine that will reap consistent rewards. The easy instructions and proven tips given here will help ensure that whatever you write is *clear*, *correct*, and *consistent*—the essential Three Cs of good communication.

What Is Proofreading?

At its most basic, proofreading means reading a piece of writing very carefully, word for word. When you sit down to proofread your final draft, look for errors in:

- **Spelling.** Choose one dictionary to use (print or online), and look up any and all words you're unsure of.

- **Grammar and usage.** Following accepted grammar rules means that your writing is presented in a way that your readers will be familiar with and be receptive to. As with spelling, take the time to look up any grammar or usage point that you're unsure of.

- **Punctuation.** Punctuation marks are like road signs—there to guide the readers to hear what you say in the way you want them to. Be sure punctuation is accurate so it helps the readers understand clearly what you're saying, with all the pauses and emphasis you intend.

- **Capitalization.** Be sure capitalization is used where it should be and isn't overused in a way that distracts the readers and calls extra attention to items that don't need to be highlighted.

- **Numerical or alphabetical sequence.** If you have anything listed in numerical or alphabetical order—like a list of items or your bibliography—ensure items are in the order they should be.

- **Formatting.** All "elements" should be used consistently—for example, all paragraphs indented the same, all page numbers in the same place on the page.

- **Consistency.** Ensure that whatever decisions you've made are presented consistently—for example, all numbers spelled out, *website* always lowercased and one word.

- **Sense and readability.** If you have to read anything more than once to understand it, then it probably could benefit from being written more clearly.

Alert

Never, ever assume. Don't presume something questionable is correct. For *anything* you're unsure of, take the time to stop and look it up.

Extra Help

Before you begin proofreading an electronic document, preserve the original and create your working copy by saving it as a new file with an altered file name. This way, if you accidentally change or delete something you didn't mean to, you have the original version as a reference.

Checking the Three Cs

Every proofread has the same aim—to make sure the finished writing and its presentation on the page are *clear*, *correct*, and *consistent*. There are some simple procedures to help you do that.

Consider a Style Sheet

A style sheet is simply a list, usually alphabetical, of anything you want to keep consistent in a piece of writing. Will you use *OK* or *okay*, *Web* or *web*, *five* or *5*? All are legitimate, but you need to pick one form and use it wherever that term appears throughout a document. You can add words, abbreviations, numbers, punctuation conventions, and anything else that could be done more than one way, or anything that you just want to remember.

For a short piece of writing like an essay, a style sheet is not vital, but if you are writing a long piece, it can be an important tool, saving you time and ensuring consistency in your writing.

Consider a Checklist

In addition to or instead of a style sheet, it's helpful to have a checklist to remind you of what to look for as you proofread. Items on your list would be similar to those mentioned in Chapter 9, but they might also be items you have changed your mind about in one place and you want to make sure you change everywhere—like the spelling or capitalization of a name. You can make your own checklist, or use one prepared by a professional and adapt it to your needs.

Extra Help

As you proofread, when you come to a word, phrase, or grammar rule you want to look up, instead of stopping to look it up, flag it in some way and look up all items at once. This way you don't break the flow of your reading.

Proofread in Stages

Just as you should review and revise your final draft in stages, the best way to ensure a thoroughly checked, consistent piece of writing is to proofread it systematically, in stages. When you pay attention to just one element at a time you'll catch more mistakes.

For proofreading long pieces of writing, we recommend an Eight Stages of Proofreading process, the guidelines of which can be found in Appendix E: Proofreading in Stages. For proofreading your essay, however, following these steps may be just what you need.

1. First, carefully read the text of the document, word for word, checking for and correcting errors in spelling, grammar, punctuation, and consistency. Also, as you read, ask yourself, "Does this make sense?" If something doesn't, take the time to fix it.

   As you come to words, phrases, grammar rules, facts, or anything else that you need to look up, don't stop reading to look them up. Instead, highlight them in some way to look up later. This way you won't lose the flow of what you're reading, and you'll be able to see the material in the way your readers will.

2. Now take the time to look up all the items you noted. If you find something that needs to be changed, change it immediately. If it's something you think needs to be changed in more than one place in your essay, take the time to change it everywhere. The Find and Replace feature in word-processing programs is immensely helpful for this part of the process.

3. Look through the whole document one more time, just to be sure there's nothing visually jarring or obviously out of place. Run a final spell-check, and in web documents, make sure all the navigation tools work.

Extra Help

If possible, ask someone else—someone with good spelling and grammar skills who is detail oriented—to proofread your essay for you. When you've looked at a piece of writing over and over, you tend to see what you expect to see and don't always see what's actually there. If you don't have someone qualified to proofread your essay for you, that's okay. Just take your time, pay close attention, look up anything you're unsure of, and you'll do a great job.

Practice Proofreading

Test your proofreading skills by correcting the errors and inconsistencies in the following memo. See the Answer Key at the end of this book for the correct answers.

Curent social, economic, and political circumstances have created more job opportunties for employees' fluent in more than one language. At the same time unfortunately due to a lack of funding, many colleges have been forced to eliminate some of their language learning classes.

PDU recently asked students to indicate which class times they would prefer for language-learning classes. The result follows:

1. 7:00 A.M.–8:00 A.M. (M–F 39.2%)

2 6:00 P.M.–7:00 P.M. M–F 10.4%)

3. 9:00 A.M.–10:00 A.M. (Saturday, 26.8%)

An additional 23,6% indicated other times, including Sunday mornings, Sunday evenings. and Saturday evenings.

With these results, the college determined they would hold language-leaming classes each weekday from 7 A.M. to 8 A.M. and Saturdays from 9 A.M. to 10 A.M.

A Final Word

Proofreading is all about details, about getting the little things right. When you do, those little things can add up to something big—writing that's memorable for all the right reasons and none of the wrong ones.

11

A Finished Assignment: From Beginning to End

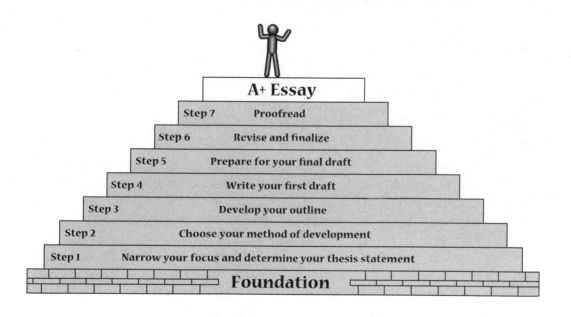

A+ Essay

Step 7	Proofread
Step 6	Revise and finalize
Step 5	Prepare for your final draft
Step 4	Write your first draft
Step 3	Develop your outline
Step 2	Choose your method of development
Step 1	Narrow your focus and determine your thesis statement

Foundation

This chapter shows you the final product—an example of a finished assignment from beginning to end. It takes you through each step so you can see what we did, how we executed the step, and what we finally produced. Here are the steps you'll see involved in developing the final essay:

- First free writing
- Research
- Second free writing
- Outline
- First draft
- Preparing for the final draft
- Final polished essay

Sample Essay

Situation: The teacher has assigned me an essay.
Prompt: Compare two possible pets and decide which one you would rather have.
Method of Development: Comparison/contrast

First Free Writing

I come home, pull out my laptop, get comfortable, and set the timer for a ten-minute free writing:

Well, I'm not sure about this. Since my mothr has always frowned on talks about pets, I never considered it would be possible to have one, but if I coud have a pet I guess I'd like to have something exotic, not the ordinary pet. I've always liked llamas and I think to be the only one around to have a llama would be pretty neat. I don't know for sure what I'd do with one because you can't ride it and it need space to roam, but we do have a big back yard. Still, I don't think a llama would be much company. Then, I've always oved koala bears and I even got to hold one when we went to Australia. He was pretty neat but his fur wasn't as soft as I thought it would be. I also heard that koalas are not as cute when you have to deal with them. They have sharp claws and sleep most of the time. I guess what I'm trying to figure out with a pet is what I want out of owning one. It seems my friends with dogs and cats are happy with them, but they also seem to take a lot of time and money and I don't know if mother would let me spend my monty on something like a pet but I guess if I earned th emone myself and then I could use it onw hat I want to but if I had to work to keep a pet I'm not sure that would be what I would want to do. Pets are sup-posed to comfort me but I don't see how comfortable I would be with having to get a job just to support a pet. Besides I'm just entering high school and I don't think iwant to take time to work. I'll have lost more homework and there are so many activities at school that I might want to get into that I can't see giving all of that up to get a job and support a pet. Still I have to come up with some-thing because the paper s due in a week and I would really like to do sompthing spectacular but I simply can't think of what that would be, so I guess I need to look around some more. I could always get a goldfish which wouln't take much time or money, but not sure a goldfish would be much company and I don't know what I could compare tha to. I turtle maybe, but that doesn't sound very ecxciting. I'll probably cave and write about dogs and cats. Even if that is not very exciting maybe I can find a way of presenting it that will make it a good paper, but I'd still rather hava a llama, but again what could I compare that to. A horse maybe? But, aain, that would take so much more researchy and I'm not sure I want to to that. There are other animals. I know someone who has a fer-ret and someone else who has a rt. Then, there are rabbits, but, aside from the llama, those are not pets I would want to have because thery'e not comforthing or loveable at lest to my mind. I guess what I feel is that is I had a pet, I would want one that gives me some comfort and that I could really love and interact with. Which brings me back to dogs and cats. If I do a good job on those two, I could still write a good paper and impress the teacher with my skill in putting my ideas on paper. That would be comforting also and I would't need to have a pet to get that sort of comfort

Research

Well—that is a start. I think I narrowed the topic down to dogs and cats at least, and now I need to do a little research to see what comparisons and contrasts I can make.

I start by talking to friends who tell me of their experiences with their pets, and I talk to my friend Nancy who has both. Next, I call the SPCA to see how much it costs to get an animal from a shelter. After that, I go to the store to get prices on food and accessories. It is amazing how much information I can find with just a little work.

Second Free Writing

A couple of days later, I look over all my information, check my first free writing, and feel I am ready to do my second free writing. I set the timer for fifteen minutes and go to work.

Well, I've narrowed the subject down and I'm sure I can do it on the difference in owning a cat or a dog. One of the things that convinced me to do this was how well I know Nancy, my friend, and her dog Angela and her Siamese cat Jasmin. That gave me a good start because I felt omfortable when I knew I would be wrigin about something that I was knowledgable about. After my research I discovgered that it wad not free to et a pet from shelter. Thyey want you to have a pet with all its shots and it should be spayed or neuteree and the prospective owner had to pay for all that. For a regular animal, with no papers, it can cost abou $200. I was shocked. Nancy got Angela, who is a minature Italian greyhound from a recue organization and she paid $1,500 for her. I would never do that. Although Angela is pretty cute and loes me a lot and I can certainly see why someone would want to have a pet that was always happy to see them and jumped all over and showed how much they loved you. Nancy's cat, Jasmin, is not the loveable kind. Most Siamese are not loveable, but they wur are pretty. I don't know if pretty is a good reason to have a pet,but Jasmin does sit on my lap and purrs and that makes me feel pretty good. I didn't realize how much work was involved to get that happy baqrk or that loving purr. As I talked to more people who have pets I discovered that there was a lot more to owning an animal than walking a dog or changing a cat's litter box. I read a little about pet owner4ship on the internet and found out a lot about things people have to do for their pets. Im not sure I would want to do all those things. When I come hom4 from school I just want to rest, and ot have to think about anything else. Then, there's all the homework I have to do and how would I get that done om my schedule if I had a pet I had to deal with. But having a pet is not an options for this paper. The option is not getting a pet but what pet I would get if I did get one. I guess if I take my elf kind of out of it all and just pretend that I will be making this decision, I can do the paper and not get the pet. Although, when I go to Nancy's and Angel jumps up and licks my face....

Outline

When I look at this second rewrite a day later, it seems pretty clear where I am going. With the research and personal experiences of my friends, I will stick to the dog/cat comparison. Now I need to find the three points I can develop and put together a simple outline. Since the teacher does not require that we hand in an outline, I will be doing this for myself.

Introduction (I want to start with some action to get my reader involved). My thesis statement will be: "I can see both pluses and minuses for choosing a dog or a cat."

   I. Costs
  II. Responsibilities
 III. Rewards

That's a pretty simple outline, but it is enough for me to get started. I go back and add three points in each paragraph to give me more of a structure and keep me on track. I come up with this extended 1-2-3.

    I. Introduction
   II. Costs
      1. Initial cost
      2. Food and accessories
      3. Maintenance
  III. Responsibilities
      1. Exercise
      2. Waste
      3. Accidents
  IV. Rewards
      1. Comfort
      2. Unconditional love
      3. Convenience
   V. Conclusion

Now that I have all the elements laid out, I should be able to fill in the blanks and tie it all together.

First Draft

With my new outline it should be easy enough to write about 500 words. Since I have been thinking about it a lot, I'm pretty ready to jump into my first draft. I want to get all the information down in an orderly fashion and then work to make the essay lively and, perhaps, give a prospective pet owner something to think about. Here's my first draft.

What's Your Pleasure?

I opened the door and Angela ran yapping to greet me, jumping up to kiss me. Nancy's miniature grayhound seems to love me as much as she does Nancy. Later, sitting and talking, her Siamese cat, Jasmine, curled up in my lap purring as I stroked her soft brown fur. Mother has finally agreed to let me get a pet of my own, and I'm torn between a dog and a cat. I can see both pluses and minuses for choosing a dog or a cat.

Cost might be a factor, but if I get a pet from the animal shelter, the initial cost would be about the same. It costs about $200 to adopt an animal from a shelter with its shots. And money doesn't stop there. Both need food, which costs about $2 a can for dogs or cats. Also, cats need kitty litter, need a pooper scooper of some kind. Annual shots for each cost about the same, so on a monetary basis there's no clear choice.

As mother keeps reminding me, there's lots of responsibilities to having a pet. Dogs need to be walked for exercise and to do their "business." Walking them can be fun, and give me lots of good exercise, also. The downside of that is that I'd have to scoop the "business," and I don't much like that. Cats don't need to be walked, and they can be trained to use a litter box. Although that sounds some better, I'd still have to clean out the litter box every day. Unfortunately, both, sometimes, have "accidents," and I hate the idea of cleaning up after a pet. Again, there's not much difference in responsibilities, except between walking and cleaning a litter box.

The big difference, finally, comes down to what I want from a pet. I want comfort. When Jasmine sits on my lap I feel relaxed and happy. Of course, Angela's frantic joy when she sees me makes me feel loved. In a world where we face trouble and rejection, the unquestioned love of an animal comforts us. If I have to be away, I can find someone to take care of a cat more easily. A cat can be fed once a day and dry food left out for later. A dog needs to be fed twice a day and you can't leave extra food out, because a dog will gobble it all up. Although the responsibility might seem a lot, I can learn from taking care of a pet. Ultimately, I'm rewarded by someone who also loves me, doesn't scold me, and always greets me lovingly.

I finally told Mom I wanted a cat. A dog can be more friendly and more enthusiastically loving, but they take more work. Ultimately, what decided me was doggie poop. I can't stand the thought of picking it up!

Preparing for the Final Draft

Taking all I know, I now review my first draft to determine what I need to revise—and finalize. Here's my thought process on different aspects of my first draft.

What's Your Pleasure?

(**Title:** I like this—it doesn't give away too much but ultimately refers to my essay.)

(**Introductory paragraph:** I think this works. It uses vivid images and is specific.)

I opened the door and Angela ran yapping to greet me, jumping up to kiss me. Nancy's miniature grayhound seems to love me as much as she does Nancy. Later, sitting and talking, her Siamese cat, Jasmine, curled up in my lap purring as I stroked her soft brown fur. Mother has finally agreed to let me get a pet of my own, and I'm torn between a dog and a cat. I can see both pluses and minuses for choosing a dog or a cat.

(**Thesis statement:** This clearly shows comparison/contrast and has the controlling idea of *choosing* and the subject of *dog or a cat*.)

(**First developmental paragraph:** It has a clear topic sentence and all the facts but does not flow very well. I'll probably have to redo it. The paragraph does have three points.)

Cost might be a factor, but if I get a pet from the animal shelter, the initial cost would be about the same. It costs about $200 to adopt an animal from a shelter with its shots. And money doesn't stop there. Both need food, which costs about $2 a can for dogs or cats. Also, cats need kitty litter, need a pooper scooper of some kind. Annual shots for each cost about the same, so on a monetary basis there's no clear choice.

(**Second developmental paragraph:** It also has a clear topic sentence and adequate development, but needs to be more specific.)

As mother keeps reminding me, there's lots of responsibilities to having a pet. Dogs need to be walked for exercise and to do their "business." Walking them can be fun, and give me lots of good exercise, also. The downside of that is that I'd have to scoop the "business," and I don't much like that. Cats don't need to be walked, and they can be trained to use a litter box. Although that sounds some better, I'd still have to clean out the litter box every day. Unfortunately, both, sometimes, have "accidents," and I hate the idea of cleaning up after a pet. Again, there's not much difference in responsibilities, except between walking and cleaning a litter box.

(**Third developmental paragraph:** It should be the strongest and it isn't quite. The topic sentence is okay, but I'm not happy with it—it doesn't seem strong enough to be the last point I leave the reader with. Need to jazz it up some.)

The big difference, finally, comes down to what I want from a pet. I want comfort. When Jasmine sits on my lap I feel relaxed and happy. Of course, Angela's frantic joy when she sees me makes me feel loved. In a world where we face trouble and rejection, the unquestioned love of an animal comforts us. If I have to be away, I can find someone to take care of a cat more easily. A cat can be fed once a day and dry food left out for later. A dog needs to be fed twice a day and you can't leave extra food out, because a dog will gobble it all up. Although the responsibility might seem a lot, I can learn from taking care of a pet. Ultimately, I'm rewarded by someone who also loves me, doesn't scold me, and always greets me lovingly.

(**Conclusion:** This kind of says what I want to say, but I'd like it to be more memorable so readers clearly see why I made my decision.)

I finally told Mom I wanted a cat. A dog can be more friendly and more enthusiastically loving, but they take more work. Ultimately, what decided me was doggie poop. I can't stand the thought of picking it up!

Final Polished Essay

Okay, I think I have all the information in a pretty good order, and I've done my proofreading. I'm pretty happy with my introduction, but the essay lacks zip. I think I need to work on better specifics and a more varied vocabulary.

So, after all this, here's my final draft. Although I don't know exactly when I will get a pet, it has been fun looking into what is involved and, when

I do get a pet, I will have already looked more carefully at the advantages that would suit me.

What's Your Pleasure?

I opened the door and Angela ran, yapping, to greet me, jumping up to kiss me. Nancy's miniature greyhound seems to love me as much as she does Nancy. Later, as we sat and talked, Nancy's Siamese cat, Jasmine, curled up in my lap, purring as I stroked her soft brown fur. I've wanted a pet of my own for years and Mother has finally agreed, but I need to decide whether a cat or a dog would be best for me.

Cost is certainly a consideration. I would probably get a pet from a shelter, but that still costs money. Friends who have adopted pets say they had to pay about $200, which includes the cost of shots and having the pet spayed or neutered. Cost does not stop there. Pets need food. I went to the supermarket to price food and found a large can of food for either is about $2. Dry food, too, costs about the same for dogs or cats. Since dogs are generally larger, they would eat more and thus be more costly. However, cats need litter, so, again, it seems the cost of owning either one would be about the same.

Having a pet involves more responsibility than money, as Mother knew when she said I couldn't have one. Dogs need to be walked for exercise twice a day to do their "business." This can be fun as you get to know other pet owners and get some good exercise. The downside is that you have to do it all the time and you also have to scoop their "business." I don't much like the thought of that. Cats, on the other hand, don't need to be walked. I've never seen a cat on a leash. They can be trained to use a litter box. Although that sounds better, I'd still have to clean the cat box every day. Unfortunately, sometimes both cats and dogs have accidents and I would have to clean those up. Depending on how much time I want to spend with my pet could influence my decision.

The decision, finally, comes down to what I want from a pet. I want comfort and companionship. When Jasmine purrs in my lap I feel relaxed and happy. Yet, Angela's frantic joy at seeing me makes me feel loved. In a world where we sometimes face trouble and rejection, the unquestioned love of an animal comforts us. But, you have to comfort the pet too. If you have to be away, getting someone to care for a cat is easier than for a dog. And then there is that twice-a-day walking. A cat can be fed once a day and dry food left out for later, but a dog needs to be fed twice a day, and you can't leave food out or he'll gobble it up. Both, however, offer unquestioned love in return for your care. A lot depends on how much time and effort you're willing to devote to pet care.

I finally told Mom that I would like to get a cat. True, a dog can be more friendly and exuberant, but I don't think I'm ready for the responsibility of a dog. Ultimately, I based my decision on the fact that I would rather change the litter box than scoop that poop.

Next Steps

We've included more examples for you to follow in Appendix F: Before and After Examples. Look through them and, with the essay here, you will have seen examples of the process from beginning to end. If you've worked through the steps of this book, you're ready to write—and write well. Congratulations, and have fun!

APPENDIX A

Checklists for Specific Essay Types

The content in this book is valuable for every essay you write—short or long, formal or informal, as a class assignment, for yourself, and for all uses.

Here is a list of items that apply to the writing of all essays, followed by checklists with additional tips to give you an extra edge when your essay has special circumstances. Finally, we include a checklist for reviewing any essay.

Checklist for All Essays—Creation and Writing

No matter the length of an essay or the time you have to complete it, there are certain elements that apply to all essays. Ask yourself these questions for all essays, in addition to considerations for particular situations.

Introduction

☐ Is the introduction 3–5 sentences?
☐ Does the introduction grab the readers' attention?
☐ Does the introduction finish with a clear thesis statement with a subject and controlling idea?

Body

☐ Are each of the three development paragraphs 10–12 sentences long?
☐ Does each paragraph begin with a clear topic sentence?
☐ Does each topic sentence clearly relate to the thesis?

☐ Does each paragraph develop three minor points to support the topic?

☐ Is there a satisfactory concluding sentence for each paragraph?

☐ Are there quotes within the body paragraphs to support my points?

☐ Can I think of any counterarguments to my own points? If so, would it strengthen my argument to voice these counterarguments and then show how my opinion is still valid?

Conclusion

☐ Is the final paragraph 3–5 sentences?

☐ Does the final paragraph restate my thesis in a new way or present a final point to round out my argument?

☐ Does the final paragraph satisfactorily end the essay and give it a note of finality?

General

☐ Have I stayed on subject throughout the essay?

☐ Have I used proper formatting?

☐ Do I use connections between sentences and paragraphs to effectively tie ideas together?

Checklists for Special Circumstances

In addition to the items noted in the previous Checklist for All Essays, consider these items when writing an essay for each of these special circumstances.

Additional Checklist for Book Reports

☐ Do I include both the title of the reference (in italics) and the name of the author in first sentence?

☐ Do I summarize the plot in 12–15 sentences?

☐ Do I check that all names and/or quotes are correct?

☐ Do I comment on what the strong points of the story are?

☐ Do I point out any weaknesses in the book?

☐ Do I discuss what message the author wants the reader to have?

☐ Do I include in the conclusion whether I would recommend the book to another reader, and why or why not?

Additional Checklist for Literature Essays

Introduction

☐ Does the introduction include background information on the author?

☐ Does the introduction include interesting events about or stories of the author that relate to the work—which often work nicely as a means of introduction?

☐ Does the thesis statement include one of these common topics as a controlling idea?
- Character development
- Evaluation of themes and motifs
- Analysis of setting/included details

Body

☐ Do I properly cite my quotations?

☐ Are transitions into and out of quotations clear?

☐ Do I avoid summarizing? (Summarizing is for book reports and should be left out of literature essays. In literature essays, the writer assumes that the reader has already read and has a basic knowledge of the book.) If I do summarize, can I replace my summary with a quotation, or can I delete it altogether because it does not serve to support my essay?

Additional Checklist for Standardized Test Essays

The first step in preparing for a standardized essay exam is to look at some model prompts and learn exactly how much time will be allotted for the essay. (Many websites and standardized test study guides have example prompts as well as examples of responses at all score levels.)

Next, practice responses to the prompts without a time limit in order to get an idea of your own style. Then look at how your responses compare to good example responses.

And finally, try at least one timed essay test to get a better idea of the amount of time you need for each aspect of the development while still leaving time at the end to review grammar and spelling.

Preparation

☐ Have I gone through my shortened prewriting (including a very brief brainstorm and writing a 1-2-3 outline to organize ideas before launching into the essay)?

Completion

☐ Does my introduction grab the readers' attention with, for example, a personal story or a well-known example?

☐ Does my introduction contain a thesis with a subject and a controlling idea that clearly asserts a position in relation to the prompt?

In the developmental paragraphs:

☐ Do I use examples from my own schoolwork or life experiences to support the position I have taken?

☐ Are there examples in literature or history that serve to support my position and also validate it by showing the presences of similar ideas in history/literature?

☐ Are there any popular culture examples that might make my point more accessible or seem more valid?

Review

☐ Have I read through my essay after completion to correct spelling and grammar errors?

The readers of standardized test essays realize that these tests are timed and view the essay presented as a rough draft, but taking the time to review your work, fix spelling errors, and correct grammar errors—which may make your essay more clear and understandable—is an easy way to improve your score and get full credit for your ideas.

Additional Checklist for College Application Essays

General

☐ Do I answer the essay question within the first paragraph?

TIP: A common question asks why you are a good fit for the college/school you are applying to or the job you are applying for.

Introduction

☐ Does my introduction grab the readers' attention?

TIP: Especially with a college application, the readers are looking at thousands of essays, so grabbing the readers' attention early is very important.

TIP: Methods include taking a controversial stance, choosing people to write about who are less mainstream (the person might even be unheard of by the readers), or taking a critical look at something not often discussed).

☐ Does the introduction finish with a thesis that either answers the question and asserts my position or presents what will be discussed as well as the opinion I hold of that topic?

☐ Does my topic include one of these common application topics:
  • A key event or events in my life
  • Times I have demonstrated leadership abilities
  • A time I have overcome a difficult situation or obstacle
  • A person who influenced me
  • Analyzing a mistake I have made in my life

Body

☐ In my developmental paragraphs, do I include proper analysis of my decisions?

☐ Can I draw on external sources to support my opinion?

☐ Are there examples to support my choices/decisions in literature? In history? In popular culture?

☐ Are there examples of people faced with similar circumstances or choices who have made the similar or different decisions, and why do these support my thesis?

☐ Are there further examples from my own life that validate my choice?

Conclusion

☐ Does my conclusion restate my thesis in a new way or present a final piece of information to round out my argument?

Review

☐ Does my essay answer the question and does my answer to the question portray me as an ideal candidate for the school/position?

☐ Does my answer make me stand out from other suitable candidates, making me the most suitable?

Checklist for All Essays—Final Review

First Read

☐ Do I have any run-on sentences?

TIP: If so, correct them, most easily with semicolons.

☐ Do I have any fragments?

TIP: If so, correct them, generally by adding the fragments to the previous or following sentences.

☐ Have I stayed in the same tense (past or present)?
☐ Do my subjects and verbs agree?
☐ Do my pronouns agree in number and gender with the nouns they replace?
☐ Is my punctuation correct?

Second Read

☐ Are there expletive sentences that need to be rewritten?
☐ Have I used specific, clear examples?
☐ Have I replaced "to be" verbs with active verbs?
☐ Am I proud of my presentation?

Grammar and Usage Glossary of Terms

Grammar Terms

adjective: a word that describes (this, that, each, such, which, five, pink, Jan's, my).

adjective clause: a subject and verb that describe (you *who writes* read a lot).

adjective phrase: a descriptive phrase (the readers with *a short attention span* looked up).

adverb: a word that describes an action (sleep *poorly*) or a description (*too* hot, *very* thin).

adverbial clause: a subject and verb that describe action (she will leave *when the rain stops*).

adverbial phrase: a phrase describing action (*after writing*, let's take a break).

agreement: the proper relation of words in a sentence—in case (between *you* and *me*), number (*her face, their faces*), and person (*I am, you are*).

case: the form of a pronoun, depending on other words used with it in the sentence (*he* took it; take it to *him*, or Dan can take it *himself*).

clause: a group of words containing a subject and verb. An independent clause can stand alone (*I am* here); a dependent (or subordinate) clause cannot (*because he sang loudly*, birds fell from the trees).

conjunction: a word that joins elements of equal value (*and, but, or, either . . . or*) or of unequal value (*when, where, before, if, for*).

dangling modifier: a word or group of words used to describe a person or thing but with an unclear reference (*being a socially responsible company*, she felt *these* standards should apply to all employees too).

gerund: a verb plus -*ing* that acts as a noun (*writing* well isn't easy).

idiomatic: a use of words peculiar to a particular language that could not be translated literally into another language (you're *pulling my leg*; let's *call it a day*).

infinitive: the base verb form, usually preceded by *to* (Meg wants *to ask* a question). An infinitive phrase is a verbal phrase introduced by an infinitive (*to hear* Joe talk, you'd think he owned the company).

noun: a name for a person, place, or thing (*book, Jose, idea*). A noun clause is a noun and verb used together as a subject or object (*when she would sign* was unknown; give it to *whoever asks* for it). A noun phrase is a group of words used as a subject or object (*finishing the book* is my goal). A collective noun refers to a group; it takes a singular verb unless its individual elements are to be emphasized (*staff, personnel, statistics*).

object, direct: the person or thing acted upon in a sentence (they sent *her* to Paris; she proofread *the manuscript*).

object, indirect: the one to or for whom the action is performed (we sent a message to *her*; leave it for *the client*).

parallelism: keeping parts of a sentence that are parallel in meaning parallel in structure (*seeing* is *believing*; *to see* is *to believe*).

participle: an *-ing* word that acts as an adjective or part of a verb (he's a *writing* fanatic; she *is writing* her first novel).

phrase: a group of words not containing a simple verb (the bird, *singing after sundown,* was thought to be a frog; the child *in the sunlight* sang to the butterflies).

preposition: a word that governs a noun or pronoun and shows position (a bird can fly *around, by, near, beside, above, over, below, under, beneath, in, into, to, toward, through, out of,* or *beyond* a cloud; *between* two clouds; *among* many clouds—*during* cloudy weather, that is).

pronoun: a word used in place of a noun, to avoid repeating it (Jenny ate fast because *she* was late; Green's has black bean soup—do you want *any*?).

pronoun, intensive: a pronoun used for emphasis (he *himself* can do it).

pronoun, reflexive: a pronoun used to turn the action back onto the subject (he burned *himself*).

subject: the key person or thing taking the action (*Ann* is here; *all pens but two* are gone).

tense: the time an action occurs. Present tense (*write, are writing*). Past tense (*wrote, were writing, had written*). Future tense (*will write, will be writing, will have written*).

verb: the action (she *is proofreading*; he *jumped*; they *came*).

voice: how the subject and verb relate. Active voice means that the subject carried out the action (Peg *ran* the press); passive voice means that the action was done to the subject (the press *was run* overnight).

Types of Sentences Based on Tone or Mood

declarative: sentences that make statements. (The managers are ethical.)

interrogative: sentences that ask questions. (Are the managers ethical?)

imperative: sentences that make demands. (The managers must be ethical!)

Types of Sentences Based on Grammatical Structure

simple: one main, or independent, clause, with any number of phrases. (I dropped the Ming vase on the floor at your house.)

compound: two or more main clauses, with any number of phrases. (I had dinner, and I dropped the Ming vase on the floor at your house.)

complex: one main clause and one or more subordinate clauses, with any number of phrases. (Before I left, but after I'd had dinner, I dropped the Ming vase on the floor.)

compound-complex: two or more main clauses and one or more subordinate clauses, with any number of phrases. (After I'd had dinner, I dropped the Ming vase on the floor at your house, and I skipped town without a word.)

Exam Essay Glossary of Terms

analyze: Take a piece of writing apart, and show how the pieces work and how they fit together well.

compare: Show the similarities between two things and explain why a similarity is important or what bearing it has on the subject.

contrast: Show the differences between two things and explain why a difference is important or what bearing it has on the subject.

describe: In specific detail, let the reader see what you see, using sensory language, such as references to sight, sound, smell, and touch.

evaluate: Make a value judgment on a subject and show why that judgment is true or not true.

identify: Show how the focus of your essay relates to the work.

prove: Form a thesis that needs to be supported, and support it clearly and logically.

summarize: In your own words, briefly recount the work your essay addresses.

Useful Word Lists

Dependent Clause Words

There are two kinds of clauses—independent and dependent. A dependent clause has the subject and verb just like an independent clause, but because it begins with a dependent word such as one in the list here, it can't stand alone; it is not a complete sentence.

> Even though I finished my homework

To make this example a complete sentence, we need to add an independent clause:

> Even though I finished my homework, I still had chores to do before I could watch TV.

after	although	as
as if	because	before
even if	even though	ever since
how	if	in order that
since	so	so that
than	that	though
unless	until	what
whatever	when	whenever
where	whereas	wherever
whether	which	whichever
while	who	whom
whose	why	

Words Most Often Misspelled

accommodate	accumulate	acknowledgment
all right	allotment	analyze
annihilate	benefit	bouillon
caffeine	colonel	conscientious
counterfeit	discipline	embarrass
entrepreneur	envelope	existence
familiar	fiery	fluorescent
foreign	harass	height
hemorrhage	innuendo	inoculate
judgment	liaison	lightning
likelihood	liquefy	maintenance
maneuver	necessary	niece
occasion	occurrence	parallel
paraphernalia	personnel	pneumonia
precede	prejudice	privilege
proceed	process	questionnaire
Realtor	receive	recommend
restaurant	rhythm	ridiculous
separate	siege	silhouette
skeptical	sophomore	spaghetti
succeed	supersede	surprise
surveillance	synonymous	thorough
tranquility	unanimous	usage
vacuum	veterinarian	waiver
weird	withheld	yield

Words Most Often Confused

The words here perplex nearly everyone from time to time. This list will help you keep them straight and use them correctly.

accept	to receive willingly
except	to exclude
advice	suggestion or counsel
advise	verb meaning "to give advice"
affect	verb meaning "to influence"
effect	noun meaning "result"; verb meaning "to bring about"
aggravate	to make worse
irritate	to annoy

all ready	prepared
already	previously
anxious	to anticipate with uneasiness
eager	to anticipate with enthusiasm
appraise	to place a value on something
apprise	to inform
awhile	"wait awhile"
a while	"wait for a while"
biweekly	every two weeks
semiweekly	twice a week
bring	action toward you: "bring it to me"
take	action away from you: "take it to him"
can	ability
may	possibility or permission
choose	to pick (in the present)
chose	picked (in the past)
climactic	refers to the high point, or culmination
climatic	refers to the weather
cite	to quote
site	location
compliment	praise
complement	something that completes, or makes perfect
comprise	to include; the whole comprises the parts
compose	to be made of; whole is composed of the parts
conscience	sense of morality
conscious	aware
convince	create or change a belief (use with "of")
persuade	motivate to take an action (use with "to")
desert	dry, sandy area
dessert	sweet dish at the end of a meal
discreet	circumspect, judicious
discrete	separate, individual

e.g.	"for example"
i.e.	"that is"
ensure	to make certain
insure	to obtain insurance; to guarantee protection or safety
everyday	one word when used as an adjective
every day	each day
farther	at a greater distance
further	in addition to
faze	to disturb or disconcert
phase	period or cycle
flair	special talent
flare	sudden bright light, or an outward spread
flaunt	to show something off
flout	to ignore or disdain
flier	one who flies
flyer	an advertising circular
home (in)	zero in on a target
hone	sharpen
imply	to hint or suggest ("he implied it to me")
infer	to deduce ("I inferred his meaning")
its	belonging to it
it's	contraction of "it is"
later	afterward
latter	the second of two things
lay	to place or put down
lie	to recline
less	for things you can't count individually ("less money")
fewer	for things you can count individually ("fewer dollars")
lets	allows
let's	contraction of "let us"
loose	not tight
lose	opposite of win

nauseous	causes nausea ("a nauseous smell")
nauseated	feel sick to one's stomach ("I'm nauseated")
passed	verb—past tense of "pass"
past	noun—the time before now
predominant	adjective meaning "prevailing"
predominate	verb meaning "to exert control over"
principal	main
principle	rule
stanch	stop the flow
staunch	faithful
stationary	not moving
stationery	paper products
than	compares
then	subsequent action
their	possessive of "they"
there	in that place
they're	contraction of "they are"
to	toward
too	also; extremely
whose	shows ownership
who's	contraction of "who is" or "who has"
your	belonging to you
you're	a contraction of "you are"

Cure for Common Words[*]

Many of us tend to use the same words over and over. Even though it is estimated that the average person knows more than 20,000 words, he or she uses only about 10 percent of those in daily life. Often it's out of habit or because it's easier to use the same words, but sometimes it's because we don't fully understand the nuance of some alternative words or when it might be appropriate—and more powerful—to use them.

---

[*]Adapted from K.D. Sullivan, *A Cure for the Common Word*, McGraw-Hill, 2007.

Granted, sometimes a vague or ambiguous word is just what you want—for example, when you are being discreet or want to leave your words open to interpretation. If friends set you up on a less-than-stellar blind date, you can gracefully get out of giving a negative opinion perhaps by vaguely describing your date as a "nice" guy.

If you do want to be specific, then begin by expanding your repertoire of words. When you write and speak you will be able to use the most precise word for your meaning, not just the first word that comes to mind. And by using these more precise words, you will be able to communicate exactly what you mean and will do so in a quick and concise manner.

Following are 35 common verbs and adjectives with their meanings, part of speech, and a host of alternative words you might use to improve the impact of your writing.

amazing (adjective): causing great surprise or sudden wonder. affecting, alarming, astonishing, astounding, bewildering, blown away, dazzling, dumbfounding, electrifying, flabbergasting, impressive, moving, overwhelming, perplexing, remarkable, shocking, staggering, startling, striking, stunning, stupefying, touching, unexpected

awesome (adjective): very impressive; inspiring; terrific; extraordinary. alarming, astonishing, awe-inspiring, awful, beautiful, breathtaking, daunting, dreadful, exalted, fabulous, fearful, fearsome, formidable, frantic, frightening, grand, horrifying, imposing, impressive, intimidating, magnificent, majestic, mind-blowing, moving, nervous, outstanding, overwhelming, shocking, striking, stunning, stupefying, stupendous, terrible, terrifying, wonderful, wondrous

bad (adjective): of poor or inferior quality; defective; deficient. abominable, amiss, atrocious, awful, bad news, beastly, bummer, careless, cheap, corrupt, crummy, defective, deficient, disagreeable, dissatisfactory, dreadful, erroneous, faulty, harmful, imperfect, inadequate, incorrect, inferior, injurious, lousy, off, offensive, poor, repulsive, rough, sad, skuzzy, sleazy, slipshod, stinking, substandard, unacceptable, unfavorable, unsatisfactory

beautiful (adjective): having qualities that give great pleasure or satisfaction to see, hear, think about; delighting the senses or mind. alluring, angelic, appealing, attractive, beauteous, bewitching, charming, classy, comely, cute, dazzling, delicate, delightful, divine, elegant, enticing, excellent, exquisite, fair, fascinating, fine, foxy, good-looking, gorgeous, graceful, grand, handsome, ideal, lovely, magnificent, marvelous, pleasing, pretty, radiant, ravishing, refined, resplendent, shapely, splendid, statuesque, stunning, sublime, superb, taking, wonderful

begin (verb): to perform the first or earliest part of some action; to commence; to start. activate, break ground, bring about, cause, commence, create, effect, embark on, enter on, enter upon, establish, eventuate, found, generate, get going, inaugurate, induce, initiate, instigate, institute, introduce, launch, lead, make, make active, motivate, mount, occasion, open, originate, plunge into, prepare, produce, set about, set up, trigger, undertake

big (adjective): large, as in size, height, width, or amount. ample, brimming, bulky, burly, chock-full, colossal, considerable, copious, enormous, extensive, fat, full, gigantic, heavy-duty, heavyweight, hefty, huge, hulking, humungous, husky, immense, jumbo, king-sized, mammoth, massive, monster, oversize, roomy, sizable, spacious, strapping, stuffed, substantial, thundering, vast, voluminous, walloping, whopping

boring (adjective): uninteresting and tiresome; dull. characterless, colorless, commonplace, drab, drag, drudging, dull, flat, ho-hum, humdrum, insipid, interminable, irksome, lifeless, monotonous, repetitious, routine, spiritless, stale, stereotypical, stodgy, stuffy, stupid, tame, tedious, threadbare, tiresome, tiring, trite, unexciting, vapid, wearisome, well-worn, zero

change (verb): to make different from what it is or from what it would be if left alone. accommodate, adapt, adjust, alter, alternate, commute, convert, diminish, diverge, diversify, evolve, fluctuate, moderate, modify, modulate, mutate, naturalize, recondition, redo, reform, regenerate, remake, remodel, renovate, reorganize, replace, resolve, restyle, revolutionize, shape, shift, substitute, tamper with, transfigure, transform, translate, transmute, transpose, turn, vacillate, vary, veer, warp

do (verb): to perform, execute, carry out. accomplish, achieve, act, arrange, bring about, cause, complete, conclude, cook, create, determine, discharge, effect, end, engage in, execute, finish, fix, fulfill, get ready, look after, make, make ready, move, operate, organize, perform, perk, prepare, produce, pull off, see to, succeed, take on, transact, undertake, wind up, work, wrap up

excellent (adjective): of the highest or finest quality; exceptionally good of its kind. accomplished, admirable, attractive, champion, choice, desirable, distinctive, distinguished, estimable, exceptional, exemplary, exquisite, fine, first, first-class, first-rate, good, great, high, incomparable, invaluable, magnificent, meritorious, notable, noted, outstanding, peerless, premium, priceless, prime, remarkable, select, skillful, splendid, sterling, striking, superb, superior, superlative, supreme, tiptop, top-notch, transcendent, unsurpassed, wonderful

exciting (adjective): producing excitement or strong feeling in; stirring; thrilling; exhilarating. animating, appealing, arousing, arresting, astonishing, bracing, breathtaking, dangerous, dramatic, electrifying, exhilarant, eye-popping, fine, flashy, heady, impelling, impressive, interesting, intoxicating, intriguing, lively, moving, neat, provocative, racy, rip-roaring, rousing, sensational, showy, spine-tingling, stimulating, stirring, thrilling, titillating, wild, zestful

good (adjective): having the qualities that are desirable or distinguishing in a particular thing; skilled. able, accomplished, adept, capable, clever, competent, efficient, experienced, expert, first-rate, masterful, proficient, proper, qualified, reliable, responsible, satisfactory, serviceable, skillful, suitable, suited, talented, thorough, trained, trustworthy, useful

great (adjective): important; eminent; distinguished; remarkable or outstanding. capital, celebrated, chief, commanding, dignified, distinguished, eminent, exalted, excellent, famous, glorious, grand, heroic, highly regarded, honorable, idealistic, illustrious, impressive, leading, lofty, lordly, magnanimous, major, noble, notable, noted, outstanding, paramount, primary, principal, prominent, puissant, regal, remarkable, renowned, royal, stately, sublime, superior, superlative, talented

happy (adjective): enjoying or showing joy or pleasure or good fortune. blissful, blithe, captivated, cheerful, chipper, content, convivial, delighted, delightful, ecstatic, elated, exultant, flying high, gay, glad, gleeful, gratified, intoxicated, jolly, joyous, jubilant, laughing, light, lively, merry, mirthful, overjoyed, peaceful, peppy, perky, playful, pleasant, pleased, satisfied, sparkling, sunny, thrilled, tickled pink, up, upbeat

hard (adjective): difficult to do or accomplish; fatiguing; troublesome. arduous, backbreaking, bothersome, burdensome, complex, complicated, demanding, distressing, exacting, exhausting, fatiguing, formidable, grinding, hairy, harsh, heavy, herculean, intricate, involved, irksome, knotty, laborious, mean, merciless, onerous, operose, rigorous, rough, rugged, serious, severe, slavish, sticky, strenuous, terrible, tiring, toilsome, tough, troublesome, unsparing, wearing, wearisome

help (verb): to give aid; to be of service or advantage; to assist. accommodate, advocate, aid, assist, back, befriend, benefit, bolster, boost, cheer, cooperate, encourage, endorse, further, intercede, patronize, plug, promote, push, relieve, root for, sanction, save, second, serve, stand by, stimulate, support, sustain, uphold

important (adjective): substantial; of much or great significance or consequence. big-league, chief, considerable, conspicuous, critical, crucial, decisive, earnest, essential, exceptional, exigent, extensive, far-reaching, foremost, front-page, grave, great, heavy, imperative, importunate, influential, large, marked, material, meaningful, momentous, notable, of substance, paramount, ponderous, pressing, primary, principal, relevant, salient, serious, signal, significant, something, standout, substantial, urgent, vital, weighty

interesting (adjective): arousing the curiosity or engaging the attention. absorbing, affecting, alluring, amusing, arresting, captivating, charismatic, compelling, curious, delightful, elegant, enchanting, engaging, engrossing, entertaining, enthralling, entrancing, exceptional, exotic, fascinating, gracious, gripping, impressive, inspiring, intriguing, inviting, magnetic, pleasing, pleasurable, provocative, refreshing, riveting, stimulating, stirring, striking, suspicious, thought-provoking, unusual, winning

kind (adjective): of a good or benevolent nature or disposition. affectionate, altruistic, amiable, amicable, benevolent, big, charitable, compassionate, congenial, considerate, cordial, courteous, friendly, generous, gentle, good-hearted, gracious, humane, humanitarian, indulgent, kindhearted, kindly, lenient, loving, mild, neighborly, obliging, philanthropic, softhearted, sympathetic, tender-hearted, thoughtful, tolerant, understanding

mean (adjective): hostile, offensive, selfish, or unaccommodating; nasty; malicious. bad-tempered, callous, cantankerous, churlish, contemptible, dangerous, despicable, difficult, dirty, disagreeable, dishonorable, evil, formidable, hard, hard-nosed, ignoble, ill-tempered, infamous, lousy, malicious, malign, nasty, pesky, rotten, rough, rude, rugged, scurrilous, shameless, sinking, snide, sour, treacherous, troublesome, ugly, unfriendly, unpleasant, unscrupulous, vicious

next (adjective): immediately following in time, order, or importance. abutting, adjacent, adjoining, after, alongside, attached, beside, bordering, close, closest, coming, connecting, consecutive, consequent, contiguous, ensuing, following, immediate, later, nearby, nearest, neighboring, proximate, subsequent, succeeding, thereafter, touching

nice (adjective): pleasing and agreeable in nature. admirable, agreeable, amiable, attractive, becoming, charming, commendable, considerate, copacetic, cordial, courteous, cultured, delightful, favorable, friendly, genial, gentle, good, gracious, helpful, ingratiating, inviting, kind, kindly, lovely, obliging, pleasant, pleasurable, polite, seemly, unpresumptuous, welcome, well-mannered, winning

part (noun): a portion or division of a whole that is separate or distinct. allotment, bit, chunk, component, constituent, department, detail, division, element, factor, fraction, fragment, helping, hunk, ingredient, installment, item, limb, lot, measure, member, module, molecule, parcel, particle, piece, portion, ration, scrap, section, sector, segment, share, side, slice, sliver, splinter, subdivision, unit

perfect (adjective): entirely without any flaws, defects, or shortcomings. absolute, accomplished, adept, beyond compare, blameless, consummate, without defect, excellent, excelling, experienced, expert, faultless, finished, flawless, foolproof, ideal, immaculate, impeccable, indefectible, masterful, masterly, matchless, peerless, pure, skilled, sound, splendid, spotless, stainless, sublime, superb, supreme, unblemished, unequaled, unmarred, untainted, untarnished

pleasant (adjective): socially acceptable or adept; polite; amiable; agreeable. affable, agreeable, amiable, amusing, bland, charming, cheerful, cheery, civilized, congenial, convivial, cordial, delightful, diplomatic, enchanting, engaging, enjoyable, fine, friendly, fun, genial, genteel, good-humored, gracious, gratifying, jolly, jovial, kindly, likable, lovely, mild-mannered, nice, obliging, pleasing, pleasurable, polite, refreshing, satisfying, sweet, sympathetic, welcome

problem (noun): situation, matter, or person that presents perplexity or difficulty. challenge, complication, dilemma, disagreement, dispute, doubt, headache, hitch, issue, mess, obstacle, pickle, predicament, quandary, question, scrape, squeeze, trouble

short (adjective): abridged; brief or concise. abbreviated, bare, boiled-down, brief, compressed, concise, condensed, curtailed, cut short, decreased, diminished, fleeting, lessened, little, momentary, pithy, pointed, precise, succinct, summarized, summary, terse, undersized, unsustained

small (adjective): of limited size; of comparatively restricted dimensions; not big. baby, bantam, bitty, cramped, diminutive, humble, immature, inadequate, inconsequential, inconsiderable, insignificant, insufficient, limited, little, meager, microscopic, mini, miniature, minuscule, minute, modest, narrow, paltry, petite, petty, pint-sized, pitiful, pocket-sized, poor, puny, scanty, short, slight, small-scale, stunted, teeny, toy, trifling, trivial, undersized, wee, young

special (adjective): distinguished or different from what is ordinary or usual. characteristic, chief, choice, defined, definite, designated, different, distinctive, exceptional, exclusive, express, extraordinary, festive, first, gala, important, individual, limited, main, major, marked, memorable, momentous, particular, peculiar, personal, primary, rare, red-letter, reserved, restricted, select, set, significant, smashing, specialized, specific, uncommon, unique, unusual

stay (verb): to spend some time in a place, in a situation, or with a person or group. abide, bide, continue, dally, delay, endure, halt, hang, hang about, hang around, hang in, hang out, hover, lag, last, linger, loiter, nest, outstay, pause, perch, procrastinate, remain, reside, respite, roost, settle, sit tight, sojourn, stand, stay put, stick around, stop, tarry

strange (adjective): deviating; unusual, extraordinary, or curious; odd. aberrant, abnormal, astonishing, astounding, atypical, bizarre, curious, different, eccentric, erratic, exceptional, extraordinary, fantastic, far-out, funny, idiosyncratic, ignorant, inexperienced, irregular, marvelous, mystifying, new, newfangled, odd, oddball, off, offbeat, outlandish, out-of-the-way, peculiar, perplexing, quaint, rare, remarkable, unaccustomed, uncanny, uncommon, unfamiliar, unheard of, unseasoned, unusual, weird

thin (adjective): of relatively slight consistency; scant; not abundant or plentiful. bony, cadaverous, delicate, emaciated, ethereal, featherweight, fine, fragile, gangly, gaunt, haggard, lanky, lean, lightweight, meager, narrow, peaked, pinched, puny, rarefied, rickety, scrawny, shriveled, skeletal, skinny, slender, slight, slim, small, spare, spindly, starved, subtle, threadlike, twiggy, undernourished, underweight, wan, wasted

use (verb): to employ for some purpose; put into service. accept, adopt, apply, bestow, capitalize, consume, control, do with, draw on, employ, exercise, exert, exhaust, expend, exploit, govern, handle, make do, make use, make with, manage, manipulate, operate, play on, ply, practice, put forth, regulate, relate, run, run through, spend, utilize, waste, wield, work

weird (adjective): of a strikingly odd or unusual character, strange. awful, creepy, curious, dreadful, eccentric, eerie, far-out, flaky, freaky, funky, ghastly, ghostly, grotesque, haunting, horrific, kooky, magical, mysterious, occult, odd, ominous, outlandish, peculiar, secret, singular, spooky, strange, supernatural, uncanny, uncouth, unearthly, unnatural

well (adverb): in a good, proper, commendable, or satisfactory manner; excellently; skillfully. ably, accurately, adeptly, adequately, admirably, agreeably, attentively, capably, capitally, carefully, closely, commendably, competently, completely, conscientiously, correctly, effectively, efficiently, effortlessly, excellently, expertly, famously, favorably, fully, irreproachably, nicely, pleasantly, proficiently, profoundly, properly, readily, rightly, satisfactorily, skillfully, smoothly, soundly, splendidly, strongly, successfully, suitably, thoroughly

APPENDIX D

Writing, Grammar, and Word References

The Art of Styling Sentences, 5th ed. Ann Longknife and K.D. Sullivan. Barron's, 2012.

The Chicago Manual of Style: The Essential Guide for Writers, Editors, and Publishers, 16th ed. The University of Chicago Press, 2010.

A Cure for the Common Word. K.D. Sullivan. McGraw-Hill, 2007.

The Elements of Style, 3rd ed. William Strunk and E. B. White. Macmillan & Co., 1979.

Merriam-Webster's Collegiate Dictionary, 11th edition. Merriam-Webster, Inc., 2003.

The Gremlins of Grammar. Toni Boyle and K.D. Sullivan. McGraw-Hill, 2005.

Woe Is I: The Grammarphobe's Guide to Better English in Plain English, 3rd ed. Patricia T. O'Conner. Riverhead Books, 2009.

Words Fail Me: What Everyone Who Writes Should Know About Writing. Patricia T. O'Conner. Mariner Books, 2000.

Writing for Life, 2nd ed. D. J. Henry. Longman, 2010.

APPENDIX E

Proofreading in Stages

Although this full list wouldn't be necessary for an essay, you will find it helpful when proofreading a longer piece of writing with several elements, such as headings, lists of items, figures or photos with captions, and so on.

Following is the Eight Stages of Proofreading process. At first glance, it looks involved, but it's really far faster and easier than you might think. Except for the first stage, most of the stages take only a few minutes, and those few minutes can make the difference between a finished product that's *almost* error free and one that truly is.

Not all the stages will apply to every document because not every document has the same features. At each stage that does apply, be especially aware of the following:

- **Typeface, size, and placement (TSP).** In headings, titles, and other design elements, is the text bold or italic? Is the font Helvetica or Times? Is all the type sized and placed consistently and correctly?

- **Capitalization and punctuation.** Are these correct and consistent in text as well as in every heading, title, and other design element?

- **Numerical sequences and alphabetization.** In lists and other numbered or lettered items, are any skipped, repeated, or out of order? Are list and table items in alphabetical order unless another way of ordering better suits the material?

Stage 1: The Main Text

First, carefully read the text of the document, word for word, checking for and correcting errors in spelling, grammar, punctuation, and consistency.

Also, as you read, ask yourself, "Does this make sense?" If something doesn't, take the time to fix it.

Stage 2: Section Numbers and Titles

Once you've finished the first reading, go back through the document, looking only at the section (or chapter, volume, issue, and so on) numbers and titles to be sure all these elements look the same and are correct within their respective chapters or sections. Think TSP, and reread all titles for typos.

Stage 3: Text Headings

This time, look only at headings within the text (the titles that introduce the different parts of a chapter, article, and so on). These usually have different levels of importance, like the levels of an outline. Make sure all headings of the same level look the same and are free of typos.

Stage 4: Lists and Tables

On this pass, check to be sure the alignment of all list and table items and the spacing around them are consistent. In bulleted and numbered lists, make sure bullet icons and number styles are consistent and that the space after the bullet or number and before the start of the item text is consistent. Check to make sure numbering is consecutive and starts over at 1 where it should. Check that the numbers in all numbered lists align the same way vertically. Make sure all numbers are followed by the same punctuation (for example, a period or a parenthesis). For list items that are more than one line long, be sure the second and subsequent lines are indented consistently. Make sure the punctuation at the end of each list item is consistent (for example, all items end with periods, or all without).

Stage 5: Captions and Art Labels

Next, check TSP, capitalization, punctuation, and numbering of any captions or labels that appear with graphics or tables. (Captions appear above, below, or beside a piece of art, a graph, or a table. For example, *Figure 1-1: U.S. Population Growth, 2004; Table 4-1: Labor Statistics by Year.*) Check for typos. Be sure that the caption or label is the correct one for the item it describes and that if the text mentions a graphic or table, the reference is to the correct one, with the correct number. Query any apparent inaccuracies.

Stage 6: Page Numbers, Headers, and Footers

Text that identifies the document or section, the author, and/or the page number often repeats across the very top or bottom of the page. Check the TSP of any headers, footers, and page numbers, and make sure they are free of typos, are capitalized correctly, and are in the correct sequence.

Stage 7: Table of Contents

Make sure that whatever appears in the table of contents exactly matches what appears in the text and that nothing that should appear in the table of contents is omitted. Be sure the formatting of the heading levels in the table of contents accurately reflects those heading levels in the text. In electronic documents, make sure all links from the table of contents to the document sections work correctly.

Stage 8: Final Look

You're almost done! Look through the whole document again, just to be sure there's nothing visually jarring or obviously out of place. Run a final spell-check, and in web documents, make sure all the navigation tools work.

Before and After Examples

Example 1

In this example, compare the first draft and the final draft of each sentence to see how the final draft sentences have improved the effectiveness of the paragraph.

Paragraph First Draft

(1) There are a lot of students who really look forward to summer vacation and enjoying three months of no school. **(2)** Leading up to summer, they spend a lot of time counting the months and days until it finally happens and that great day arrives. **(3)** That great day finally happens and they are finally free. **(4)** At last they don't have a schedule, they don't have homework, and they don't have any responsibilities—well, no school responsibilities. **(5)** And although all these things sound wonderful, they don't know what to do with all the extra time on their hands, and, with no structure, they feel at loose ends. **(6)** If students take the time to do some planning and setting up a schedule to give them some structure to the time off, they can have a vacation that is pleasurable and useful.

Sentence 1, First Draft

There are a lot of students who really look forward to summer vacation and enjoying three months of no school.

No need for expletive sentence. Take out "there are a lot of" and replace with "many," which says the same thing in one rather than five words. Also, take out "who" and "really," which you don't need.

Sentence 1, Rewritten

Many students look forward to summer vacation and enjoying three months of no school.

Sentence 2, First Draft

Leading up to summer, they spend a lot of time counting the months and days until it finally happens and that great day arrives.

Take out "they spend a lot of time counting," which is wordy and not vital. Change to "they count," which is stronger and more active. Take out "finally happens," which is already contained in "that great day." With this wording change, "arrives" is not necessary.

Sentence 2, Rewritten

Leading up to summer, they count the months and days until that great day.

Sentence 3, First Draft

That great day finally happens and they are finally free.

No need to repeat "that great day." Replace it with the pronoun "it." You need "finally" only once in the sentence. Take out the second one, since the impact of "finally happens" is stronger.

Sentence 3, Rewritten

It finally happens and they are free.

Sentence 4, First Draft

At last they don't have a schedule, they don't have homework, and they don't have any responsibilities—well, no school responsibilities.

Sentence is wordy and cluttered. You don't need "at last," since it is basically a repeat of "finally happens." The repeat of "they don't have" takes away the force of the freedom. Replace with a simple "no."

Sentence 4, Rewritten

They have no schedule, no homework, and no responsibilities—well, no school responsibilities.

Sentence 5, First Draft

And although all these things sound wonderful, they don't know what to do with all the extra time on their hands, and, with no structure, they feel at loose ends.

You don't need "and" and "although," since they're basically the same idea. "They" is an unclear reference and seems to refer to "things." Change "they" to "some students." Take out "on their hands." It is a cliché and adds nothing. Delete the second "all"—it's unnecessary and sounds repetitive.

Sentence 5, Rewritten

Although all these things sound wonderful, some students don't know what to do with the extra time, and, with no structure, they feel at loose ends.

Sentence 6, First Draft

If students take the time to do some planning and setting up a schedule to give them some structure to the time off, they can have a vacation that is pleasurable and useful.

There are lots of extra words in this sentence. Take out "If students take the time to do" and change the weak -ing words, and the sentence becomes much stronger. You don't need "give some" since "structure" implies this. To strengthen the message, you want to leave the reader with a positive thought, so reverse last thought to "useful and pleasurable."

Sentence 6, Rewritten

If students make some plans and set up a schedule to structure the time off, they can have a vacation that is useful and pleasurable.

Paragraph Final Draft

(1) Many students look forward to summer vacation and enjoying three months of no school. **(2)** Leading up to summer, they count the months and days until that great day. **(3)** It finally happens and they are free. **(4)** They have no schedule, no homework, and no responsibilities—well, no school responsibilities. **(5)** Although all these things sound wonderful, some students don't know what to do with the extra time, and, with no structure, they feel at loose ends. **(6)** If students make some plans and set up a schedule to structure the time off, they can have a vacation that is useful and pleasurable.

Example 2

Improving this example involves both rewriting and combining sentences.

Paragraph First Draft

(1) "The Road Not Taken" is a poem by Robert Frost. **(2)** It is a poem that tells of the poet standing at a crossroad trying to decide which road to take. **(3)** One road looks less traveled. **(4)** He decides to take that road. **(5)** He tells himself that he can, maybe, take the other one some other time. **(6)** He says at the end of the poem that the road he chose made "all the difference." **(7)** He wants the reader to realize that which choice he makes has consequences.

Sentence 1, First Draft

"The Road Not Taken" is a poem by Robert Frost.

This sentence does introduce a subject but not a topic—no controlling idea. Combine it with sentence 2.

Sentence 2, First Draft

It is a poem that tells of the poet standing at a crossroad trying to decide which road to take.

Combine this sentence with sentence 1 to form a topic.

Sentences 1 and 2, Rewritten

Robert Frost's poem "The Road Not Taken" shows a person in a quandary and how he resolves the problem.

Sentence 3, First Draft

One road looks less traveled.

To fix this choppy sentence, combine it with sentences 4 and 5 to vary sentence structure and connect more clearly.

Sentence 4, First Draft

He decides to take that road.

Another short sentence; combine it with sentences 3 and 5.

Sentence 5, First Draft

He tells himself that he can, maybe, take the other one some other time.

A slightly wordy sentence; it repeats "other," and needs to be combined with sentences 3 and 4.

Sentences 3, 4, and 5, Rewritten

One road looks less traveled and, after consideration, he chooses that one. He tells himself he can, perhaps, take the more-traveled one later.

Sentence 6, First Draft

He says at the end of the poem that the road he chose made "all the difference."

Change "says at the end of the poem" to "concludes" to be more concise. Delete "that the road he chose," since "his choice" implies the road in the poem.

Sentence 6, Rewritten

He concludes that his choice "made all the difference."

Sentence 7, First Draft

He wants the reader to realize that which choice he makes has consequences.

Change the opening of the sentence from "He" to "Frost." Using the poet's name adds weight to the message. To eliminate sexist language, change "reader" to "readers" and "which choice he makes" to "the choices they make."

Sentence 7, Rewritten

Frost wants his readers to realize that the choices they make do have consequences.

Paragraph Final Draft

(1) Robert Frost's poem "The Road Not Taken" shows a person in a quandary and how he resolves the problem. **(2)** One road looks less traveled and, after consideration, he chooses that one. **(3)** He tells himself he can, perhaps, take the more-traveled one later. **(4)** He concludes that his choice "made all the difference." **(5)** Frost wants his readers to realize that the choices they make do have consequences.

Example 3

In this example, again, some sentences can be rewritten; others benefit from reducing the number of words and combining sentences.

Paragraph First Draft

(1) It was really bad when David got an F in his English class. **(2)** David had always been a good student. **(3)** The F really upset him and his parents. **(4)** They decided to go to the school counselor and see if there was anything that could be done to fix the problem. **(5)** The counselor helped them figure out what the actual problem was and also helped them set up a plan to solve the problem.

Sentence 1, First Draft

It was really bad when David got an F in his English class.

A more dynamic start would be better, so eliminate the expletive sentence "It was" and begin with "David got an F." Also, "class" isn't needed, since it is implied and adds an unnecessary word.

Sentence 1, Rewritten

David got an F in English.

Sentence 2, First Draft

David had always been a good student.

No need to repeat the name, so change "David" to "He." For sentence variety, combine sentences 2 and 3. Also, add "so" to show the relationship between the first and second parts of the new sentence.

Sentence 3, First Draft

The F really upset him and his parents.

Again, for sentence variety, combine with sentence 2 (as shown in Sentence 2, Final Draft).

Sentences 2 and 3, Rewritten

He had always been a good student, so the F really upset him and his parents.

Sentence 4, First Draft

They decided to go to the school counselor and see if there was anything that could be done to fix the problem.

The sentence is too wordy. To be more concise, change "They decided to go to" to "They went," which eliminates the weak "to go to" construction. Also, condense by changing "see if there was anything that could be done," to "for assistance."

Sentence 4, Rewritten

They went to the school counselor for assistance.

Sentence 5, First Draft

The counselor helped them figure out what the actual problem was and also helped them set up a plan to solve the problem.

No need to repeat "counselor," so change it to "She." Change "figure out what the actual problem was" to more concise language and more meaningful wording: "analyze the problem and devise a plan to improve the situation."

Sentence 5, Rewritten

She helped them analyze the problem and devise a plan to improve the situation.

Paragraph Final Draft

(1) David got an F in English. **(2)** He had always been a good student, so the F really upset him and his parents. **(3)** They went to the school counselor for assistance. **(4)** She helped them analyze the problem and devise a plan to improve the situation.

Answer Key

To ensure you won't have to go back and forth between the questions in the chapters and the answers here, we've include both.

Chapter 2

Practice Thesis Statements

The better you can identify subjects and controlling ideas in thesis statements, the easier it will be for you to write effective ones. Following are five thesis statements. Underline the subject and write S above it. Then underline the controlling idea and write C over it.

1. Recycling can make a real difference.
   Answer: The subject is "recycling," and the controlling idea is "make a difference."

2. Going green really starts at home.
   Answer: The subject is "going green," and the controlling idea is "starts at home."

3. Recycling seems to be a good idea.
   Answer: The subject is "recycling," and the controlling idea is "seems." "Seems" suggests that it might not be and could take your paper in a different direction.

4. One person can do a lot to make a difference.
   Answer: The subject is "one person," and the controlling idea is "can make."

5. More Kermits can make a greener planet.
   Answer: The subject here is a little harder. The subject in the statement is "more Kermits," but it actually refers to all animals, and the controlling idea is how this "can make a greener planet."

Chapter 3

Practice Methods of Development

To check how well you can identify the various methods of development, identify which type of essay each of these thesis statements sets up (*narration, description, process, comparison/contrast, cause and effect,* or *argument/persuasion*), and underline the key word(s) in each that lead(s) to your decision.

1. It's difficult to decide which type of exercise program is best.
   Answer: comparison/contrast

2. Schools should do more to develop students' physical development.
   Answer: argument/persuasion

3. I will always remember the sights and sounds of my first baseball game.
   Answer: description

4. Exercising can change your life in more ways than one.
   Answer: cause and effect

5. By learning these simple steps, you too can develop an effective exercise program.
   Answer: process

6. I discovered that playing sports involves more than skill.
   Answer: narration

Chapter 4

Practice Outlines

Now that you've learned how to start with an outline and develop an essay—or a paragraph—let's practice creating a brief 1-2-3 outline. Read the narration paragraph here and fill in the blanks in the outline template that follows.

I'll always remember Amsterdam. My Mom and I spent three days in Amsterdam and did most of the tourist things. We visited the Van Gogh Museum and were quite impressed. We stopped at shops and headed to the Anne Frank House. Seeing that was a remarkable experience. But what happened next was more memorable. As we walked, my Mom tripped and fell into the canal. And she doesn't swim. Fortunately, I do. I jumped in, grabbed her by the shoulders, and swam her back to the wall, where several people helped us out of the water. Mom said she was very, very glad I had been there to save her life.

I. (topic sentence): I'll always remember Amsterdam.
  A. (1st point): We did normal tourist things.
  B. (2nd point): We visited the Anne Frank House.
  C. (3rd point): My Mom fell into the canal.
II. (conclusion): My Mom was very glad I was there.

Chapter 5

Practice Topic Sentences and Possible Example Answers

As you've learned in this chapter, a topic sentence sets the tone for each developmental paragraph. Following are three thesis statements, with a brief 1-2-3 outline for each. Using these as clues to what each developmental paragraph will be about, write a topic sentence for each outline point you might use in your developmental paragraph to support the thesis statement.

Thesis statement 1: Superhero movies have a power of popularity that has lasted nearly since the beginning of film.
  A. Original *Superman* movie, 1978, big box-office hit
  B. *Batman* movies, 1943–2008, consistency in sales
  C. *Iron Man 2*, 2010, more box-office success

Thesis statement 1: Examples
  A. The original *Superman* movie, released in 1978, is an iconic super-hero movie, and upon its release it was immediately a box-office success.
  B. Based on a comic book character introduced in 1939, the *Batman* movies have consistently achieved moderate to extreme box-office success and popularity for over 70 years.
  C. *Iron Man 2* represents the new school of superhero films with more special effects, but in 2010, what remained constant was the box-office success.

Thesis statement 2: While there are some major differences between the *Harry Potter* and *Twilight* series, one of the most important contributions they both have achieved is to encourage young adults to read.

- A. *Harry Potter*, children and adults, wizardry
- B. *Twilight*, tweeners, vampire romance
- C. *Harry Potter* and *Twilight*, new generations of readers, technology generation

Thesis statement 2: Examples

- A. *Harry Potter* is a series directed toward a broad audience of both children and adults, by virtue of its wizardry and fantasy, intertwined with complex character development and situations presented.
- B. *Twilight* is aimed more exclusively at "tweeners," young women who can be absorbed in the vampire fantasy but who are also drawn in by the non-explicit romance.
- C. *Harry Potter* and *Twilight* may have their superficial differences, but for a generation mainly surrounded by technology and instant gratification, the two series introduce new readers to the power, importance, and joys of the written word.

Thesis statement 3: It is a common practice in the United States to go directly from high school to college; however, all students should be encouraged to take a year off before enrolling in college.

- A. Travel, nonbook learning, personal growth
- B. Work, privilege of attending college, value of a dollar
- C. Volunteer work, new perspectives, future planning

Thesis statement 3: Examples

- A. Taking a year off before enrolling in college can give students the opportunity to travel and experience nonbook learning, which often allows students to grow personally and enter college with a clear focus.
- B. Taking time off after high school to work can lead students to appreciate the value of their money, the value of a day's work, and the privilege they have in being able to attend college.
- C. Finally, a year off can give time to volunteer, which leads many students to gain new perspectives, as well as sometimes orienting students with regards to college majors and offering added motivation for the future.

Chapter 6

Practice Sentences

For practice, take a look at the following sentences, and underline the subject once and the verb twice. You're looking for the subject and verb only in the *independent clause*. Although the dependent clauses may have subjects and verbs, they are not complete thoughts and so are not sentences.

1. Before the football game at the stadium, we all ate dinner at Mary's.

2. The game can change in minutes because all the players are skilled.

3. Beside the pond, an egret waddled by on spindly legs.

4. Once she developed her thesis statement, the essay became easy to write.

5. He went to the soccer game even though he had lots of homework to do.

Practice Sentence Fixes

Test your ability to identify these possible missteps. In the following exercise, correct run-on sentences with a semicolon or a FANBOYS, and correct fragments by adding an independent clause. Remember—each sentence must have an independent clause.

1. They were out playing he was studying.
   Answer: They were out playing; he was studying.

2. After about 10 days in Italy.
   Answer: After about 10 days in Italy, I still found it fascinating.

3. I wanted to buy a little gondola, my mother wouldn't let me.
   Answer: I wanted to buy a little gondola, but my mother wouldn't let me.

4. After our trip, which took almost two weeks.
   Answer: After our trip, which took almost two weeks, I wanted to come home.

5. If I had only studied for that English test.
   Answer: If I had only studied for that English test I could have made an A.

Chapter 7

Practice Agreement

Accurate agreement is important not only to follow the rules but also to help the reader clearly understand your intended message. In each of the first set of sentences here, choose which underlined word accurately fits the sentence. Notice how lack of agreement can make the sentence confusing—and sometimes actually incorrect.

1. Caleb is one of those people who enjoy/enjoys reading.
   Answer: Caleb is one of those people who enjoy reading.
   (**Hint:** Rewrite like this to see if *enjoy* or *enjoys* is correct: Of those people who enjoy reading, Caleb is one.)

2. Completing/Having completed the tournament, Barbara took the next flight.
   Answer: Having completed the tournament, Barbara took the next flight.
   (**Hint:** Use the past tense if both actions were completed in the past.)

3. As the cells divide, a series of events is/are set into motion.
   Answer: As the cells divide, a series of events is set into motion.
   (**Hint:** Make verbs agree with the subject, not with a modifying phrase. In this sentence, *a series* is the subject and takes a singular verb.)

4. Coffee and milk is/are best with breakfast.
   Answer: Surprise! Either could be correct depending on your meaning. "Coffee and milk is best" indicates that you think *a combination* of coffee and milk is best.
   "Coffee and milk are best" indicates that you think both these separate drinks are best with breakfast.

5. Neither the prices nor the quality has/have changed.
   Answer: Neither the prices nor the quality has changed.
   (**Hint:** Use a plural verb after two subjects joined by *and*; use a singular verb after subjects joined by *or, nor,* or anything else.)

Now correct the following sentences so all elements are in agreement.

1. Continuous improvement means studying, practicing, and a commitment of time to your goal.
   Answer: Continuous improvement means studying, practicing, and committing time to your goal.

2. If you had asked me how I painted, I would say with bright and bold colors.
   Answer: If you had asked me how I painted, I would have said with bright and bold colors.

3. She sang louder than him.
   Answer: She sang louder than he.

Practice Punctuation

Add the missing punctuation to the following seven sentences.

1. A wonderful thing happened last night my friends gave me a surprise birthday party.
   Answer: A wonderful thing happened last night—my friends gave me a surprise birthday party.

2. If you are in a hurry use a quick drying glue for the top layer
   Answer: If you are in a hurry, use a quick-drying glue for the top layer.

3. The director Sophia lives in San Francisco but all the actors live in New York.
   Answer: The director, Sophia, lives in San Francisco, but all the actors live in New York.

4. The new manager was confident that a crisis could be averted the workers having witnessed this sort of predicament before were not so sure.
   Answer: The new manager was confident that a crisis could be averted; the workers, having witnessed this sort of predicament before, were not so sure.

5. I enjoyed the movie Chariots of Fire but some people thought it was dull
   Answer: I enjoyed the movie *Chariots of Fire*, but some people thought it was dull.

6. Not many people know that the song Happy Birthday was written in 1893.
   Answer: Not many people know that the song "Happy Birthday" was written in 1893.

7. Every question you ask should be three things clear concise and polite.
   Answer: Every question you ask should be three things: clear, concise, and polite.

Chapter 8

Practice Avoiding "To Be" Verbs

Change the following sentences by replacing the "to be" verbs with active verbs.

1. The decision to expand was made by the chairman.
   Answer: The chairman decided to expand.

2. It was late when I arrived at the bazaar.
   Answer: I arrived at the bazaar late.

3. My last exam, fortunately, was the easiest.
   Answer: I had the easiest exam last.

4. When my sister bought tickets to the concert, I was astonished.
   Answer: My sister astonished me when she bought tickets to the concert.

5. If I had known I was going to get the job, I would have bought an iPhone.
   Answer: If I had known I would get the job, I would have bought an iPhone.

Practice Passive to Active Voice and Avoiding Wordiness

Following are passive sentences that would work better as active sentences. Rewrite to change them from passive to active. Concentrate on explaining who or what performs the action. As a bonus, most often active writing uses fewer words than passive writing, thus minimizing unnecessary wordiness.

1. With the use of the right tools, the chair can be fixed quickly. (13 words)
   Possible rewrite: Use the right tools to fix the chair quickly. (9 words)

2. When a fan is moved back and forth, a pressure is produced by the motion at every point the fan passes, which is observed as a soft breeze being created. (30 words)
   Possible rewrite: The motion of a fan moving back and forth produces pressure at every point the fan passes, which creates a soft breeze. (22 words)

3. Judgment should be exercised in laying out the steps of the process so that the plan is shown as practical. (20 words)
   Possible rewrite: Exercise judgment in laying out the process steps, showing the plan as practical. (13 words)

Chapter 10

Practice Proofreading

Test your proofreading skills by correcting the errors and inconsistencies in the following memo.

Current social, economic, and political circumstances have created more job opportunities for employees fluent in more than one language. At the same time, unfortunately, due to a lack of funding, many colleges have been forced to eliminate some of their language-learning classes.

PDU recently asked students to indicate which class times they would prefer for language-learning classes. The results follow:

1. 7:00 A.M.–8:00 A.M. (M–F), 39.2%

2. 6:00 P.M.–7:00 P.M (M–F), 10.4%

3. 9:00 A.M.–10:00 A.M. (Saturday), 26.8%

An additional 23.6% indicated other times, including Saturday evenings, Sunday mornings, and Sunday evenings.

With these results, the college determined they would hold language-learning classes each weekday from 7:00 A.M. to 8:00 A.M. and Saturdays from 9:00 A.M. to 10:00 A.M.

Index